MznLnx

Missing Links Exam Preps

Exam Prep for

Algebra 2

Schultz, et al., 1st Edition

The MznLnx Exam Prep is your link from the texbook and lecture to your exams.
The MznLnx Exam Preps are unauthorized and comprehensive reviews of your textbooks.

All material provided by MznLnx and Rico Publications (c) 2010
Textbook publishers and textbook authors do not particpate in or contribute to these reviews.

MznLnx

Rico
Publications

Exam Prep for Algebra 2
1st Edition
Schultz, et al.

Publisher: Raymond Houge
Assistant Editor: Michael Rouger
Text and Cover Designer: Lisa Buckner
Marketing Manager: Sara Swagger
Project Manager, Editorial Production: Jerry Emerson
Art Director: Vernon Lowerui

Product Manager: Dave Mason
Editorial Assitant: Rachel Guzmanji
Pedagogy: Debra Long
Cover Image: Jim Reed/Getty Images
Text and Cover Printer: City Printing, Inc.
Compositor: Media Mix, Inc.

(c) 2010 Rico Publications

ALL RIGHTS RESERVED. No part of this work covered by the copyright may be reproduced or used in any form or by an means--graphic, electronic, or mechanical, including photocopying, recording, taping, Web distribution, information storage, and retrieval systems, or in any other manner--without the written permission of the publisher.

Printed in the United States
ISBN:

For more information about our products, contact us at:
Dave.Mason@RicoPublications.com

For permission to use material from this text or product, submit a request online to:
Dave.Mason@RicoPublications.com

Contents

CHAPTER 1
Data and Linear representations — 1
CHAPTER 2
Numbers and Functions — 17
CHAPTER 3
Systems of Linear Equations and Inequalities — 35
CHAPTER 4
Matrices — 48
CHAPTER 5
Quadratic Functions — 60
CHAPTER 6
Exponential and Logarirhmic Functions — 77
CHAPTER 7
Polynomial functions — 93
CHAPTER 8
Rational Functions and Radical Functions — 107
CHAPTER 9
Conic Sections — 125
CHAPTER 10
Discrete Mathematics: Counting Principles and Probability — 139
CHAPTER 11
Discrete Mathematics: Series and Patterns — 146
CHAPTER 12
Discrete Mathematics: Statistics — 154
CHAPTER 13
Trigonometric Functions — 164
CHAPTER 14
Further Topics in Trigonometry — 172
ANSWER KEY — 177

TO THE STUDENT

COMPREHENSIVE

The *MznLnx* Exam Prep series is designed to help you pass your exams. Editors at MznLnx review your textbooks and then prepare these practice exams to help you master the textbook material. Unlike study guides, workbooks, and practice tests provided by the texbook publisher and textbook authors, *MznLnx* gives you **all** of the material in each chapter in exam form, not just samples, so you can be sure to nail your exam.

MECHANICAL

The MznLnx Exam Prep series creates exams that will help you learn the subject matter as well as test you on your understanding. Each question is designed to help you master the concept. Just working through the exams, you gain an understanding of the subject--its a simple mechanical process that produces success.

INTEGRATED STUDY GUIDE AND REVIEW

MznLnx is not just a set of exams designed to test you, its also a comprehensive review of the subject content. Each exam question is also a review of the concept, making sure that you will get the answer correct without having to go to other sources of material. You learn as you go! Its the easiest way to pass an exam.

HUMOR

Studying can be tedious and dry. MznLnx's instructional design includes moderate humor within the exam questions on occassion, to break the tedium and revitalize the brain

Chapter 1. Data and Linear representations

1. Multiple Signal Classification, also known as _____, is an algorithm used for frequency estimation and emitter location.
   a. Thing
   b. Music0
   c. Undefined
   d. Undefined

2. The payment of _____ as remuneration for services rendered or products sold is a common way to reward sales people.
   a. Commission0
   b. Thing
   c. Undefined
   d. Undefined

3. The word _____ comes from the Latin word linearis, which means created by lines.
   a. Linear0
   b. Thing
   c. Undefined
   d. Undefined

4. Initial objects are also called _____, and terminal objects are also called final.
   a. Coterminal0
   b. Thing
   c. Undefined
   d. Undefined

5. U.S. liquid _____ is legally defined as 231 cubic inches, and is equal to 3.785411784 litres or abotu 0.13368 cubic feet. This is the most common definition of a _____. The U.S. fluid ounce is defined as 1/128 of a U.S. _____.
   a. Gallon0
   b. Thing
   c. Undefined
   d. Undefined

6. A _____ is a special kind of ratio, indicating a relationship between two measurements with different units, such as miles to gallons or cents to pounds.
   a. Thing
   b. Rate0
   c. Undefined
   d. Undefined

7. The _____ of a ring R is defined to be the smallest positive integer n such that $n\,a = 0$, for all a in R.
   a. Thing
   b. Characteristic0
   c. Undefined
   d. Undefined

8. A _____ is a symbolic representation denoting a quantity or expression. It often represents an "unknown" quantity that has the potential to change.
   a. Thing
   b. Variable0
   c. Undefined
   d. Undefined

9. In mathematics, a _____ may be described informally as a number that can be given by an infinite decimal representation.
   a. Real number0
   b. Thing
   c. Undefined
   d. Undefined

10. _____ is a kind of property which exists as magnitude or multitude. It is among the basic classes of things along with quality, substance, change, and relation.
    a. Amount0
    b. Thing
    c. Undefined
    d. Undefined

Chapter 1. Data and Linear representations

11. A _____ is an equation in which each term is either a constant or the product of a constant times the first power of a variable.
    a. Thing
    b. Linear equation0
    c. Undefined
    d. Undefined

12. An _____ is a collection of two not necessarily distinct objects, one of which is distinguished as the first coordinate and the other as the second coordinate.
    a. Ordered pair0
    b. Thing
    c. Undefined
    d. Undefined

13. In mathematics, the conjugate _____ or adjoint matrix of an m-by-n matrix A with complex entries is the n-by-m matrix A* obtained from A by taking the transpose and then taking the complex conjugate of each entry.
    a. Thing
    b. Pairs0
    c. Undefined
    d. Undefined

14. _____ means in succession or back-to-back
    a. Consecutive0
    b. Thing
    c. Undefined
    d. Undefined

15. In mathematics and the mathematical sciences, a _____ is a fixed, but possibly unspecified, value. This is in contrast to a variable, which is not fixed.
    a. Thing
    b. Constant0
    c. Undefined
    d. Undefined

16. _____ are the basic objects of study in graph theory. Informally speaking, a graph is a set of objects called points, nodes, or vertices connected by links called lines or edges.
    a. Thing
    b. Graphs0
    c. Undefined
    d. Undefined

17. A _____ is an individual or household that purchases and uses goods and services generated within the economy.
    a. Consumer0
    b. Thing
    c. Undefined
    d. Undefined

18. In economics, supply and _____ describe market relations between prospective sellers and buyers of a good.
    a. Demand0
    b. Thing
    c. Undefined
    d. Undefined

19. _____ is the ability to hold, receive or absorb, or a measure thereof, similar to the concept of volume.
    a. Capacity0
    b. Concept
    c. Undefined
    d. Undefined

20. _____ refers to selected population characteristics as used in government, marketing or opinion research, or the demographic profiles used in such research.

Chapter 1. Data and Linear representations

a. Thing
b. Demographics0
c. Undefined
d. Undefined

21. _____ is a physical property of a system that underlies the common notions of hot and cold; something that is hotter has the greater _____.
   a. Thing
   b. Temperature0
   c. Undefined
   d. Undefined

22. _____ is the interdisciplinary scientific study of the atmosphere that focuses on weather processes and forecasting.
   a. Meteorology0
   b. Thing
   c. Undefined
   d. Undefined

23. _____ is a temperature scale named after the German physicist Daniel Gabriel _____ , who proposed it in 1724.
   a. Thing
   b. Fahrenheit0
   c. Undefined
   d. Undefined

24. In mathematics, there are several meanings of _____ depending on the subject.
   a. Degree0
   b. Thing
   c. Undefined
   d. Undefined

25. A _____ is a set of numbers that designate location in a given reference system, such as x,y in a planar _____ system or an x,y,z in a three-dimensional _____ system.
   a. Thing
   b. Coordinate0
   c. Undefined
   d. Undefined

26. In mathematics, a _____ is a two-dimensional manifold or surface that is perfectly flat.
   a. Plane0
   b. Thing
   c. Undefined
   d. Undefined

27. A _____ is the result of the addition of a set of numbers. The numbers may be natural numbers, complex numbers, matrices, or still more complicated objects. An infinite _____ is a subtle procedure known as a series.
   a. Sum0
   b. Thing
   c. Undefined
   d. Undefined

28. In mathematics, a _____ of an integer n, also called a factor of n, is an integer which evenly divides n without leaving a remainder.
   a. Thing
   b. Divisor0
   c. Undefined
   d. Undefined

29. _____ is a synonym for information.
   a. Thing
   b. Data0
   c. Undefined
   d. Undefined

30. The _____ of measurement are a globally standardized and modernized form of the metric system.

Chapter 1. Data and Linear representations

    a. Thing
    b. Units0
    c. Undefined
    d. Undefined

31. _____ is often used to describe the measurement of the steepness, incline, gradient, or grade of a straight line. The _____ is defined as the ratio of the "rise" divided by the "run" between two points on a line, or in other words, the ratio of the altitude change to the horizontal distance between any two points on the line.
    a. Thing
    b. Slope0
    c. Undefined
    d. Undefined

32. Any point where a graph makes contact with an coordinate axis is called an _____ of the graph
    a. Thing
    b. Intercept0
    c. Undefined
    d. Undefined

33. A _____ is a quantity that denotes the proportional amount or magnitude of one quantity relative to another.
    a. Thing
    b. Ratio0
    c. Undefined
    d. Undefined

34. In mathematics, a matrix can be thought of as each row or _____ being a vector. Hence, a space formed by row vectors or _____ vectors are said to be a row space or a _____ space.
    a. Column0
    b. Concept
    c. Undefined
    d. Undefined

35. In mathematics, defined and _____ are used to explain whether or not expressions have meaningful, sensible, and unambiguous values.
    a. Thing
    b. Undefined0
    c. Undefined
    d. Undefined

36. In astronomy, geography, geometry and related sciences and contexts, a plane is said to be _____ at a given point if it is locally perpendicular to the gradient of the gravity field, i.e., with the direction of the gravitational force at that point.
    a. Thing
    b. Horizontal0
    c. Undefined
    d. Undefined

37. _____ is a term used in accounting, economics and finance with reference to the fact that assets with finite lives lose value over time.
    a. Depreciation0
    b. Thing
    c. Undefined
    d. Undefined

38. _____ is, or relates to, the _____ temperature scale .
    a. Thing
    b. Celsius0
    c. Undefined
    d. Undefined

39. Equivalence is the condition of being _____ or essentially equal.
    a. Thing
    b. Equivalent0
    c. Undefined
    d. Undefined

Chapter 1. Data and Linear representations

40. Compass and straightedge or ruler-and-compass _____ is the _____ of lengths or angles using only an idealized ruler and compass.
    a. Construction0
    b. Thing
    c. Undefined
    d. Undefined

41. An _____ is a straight line around which a geometric figure can be rotated.
    a. Axis0
    b. Thing
    c. Undefined
    d. Undefined

42. In plane geometry, a _____ is a polygon with four equal sides, four right angles, and parallel opposite sides. In algebra, the _____ of a number is that number multiplied by itself.
    a. Thing
    b. Square0
    c. Undefined
    d. Undefined

43. _____ is the distance around a given two-dimensional object. As a general rule, the _____ of a polygon can always be calculated by adding all the length of the sides together. So, the formula for triangles is P = a + b + c, where a, b and c stand for each side of it. For quadrilaterals the equation is P = a + b + c + d. For equilateral polygons, P = na, where n is the number of sides and a is the side length.
    a. Perimeter0
    b. Thing
    c. Undefined
    d. Undefined

44. A _____ is a tool similar to a ruler, but without markings.
    a. Straightedge0
    b. Thing
    c. Undefined
    d. Undefined

45. A _____ is a unit of length, usually used to measure distance, in a number of different systems, including Imperial units, United States customary units and Norwegian/Swedish mil. Its size can vary from system to system, but in each is between 1 and 10 kilometers. In contemporary English contexts _____ refers to either:
    a. Thing
    b. Mile0
    c. Undefined
    d. Undefined

46. In geometry, two lines or planes if one falls on the other in such a way as to create congruent adjacent angles. The term may be used as a noun or adjective. Thus, referring to Figure 1, the line AB is the _____ to CD through the point B.
    a. Perpendicular0
    b. Thing
    c. Undefined
    d. Undefined

47. _____ is the transport of people on a trip/journey or the process or time involved in a person or object moving from one location to another.
    a. Travel0
    b. Thing
    c. Undefined
    d. Undefined

48. The existence and properties of _____ are the basis of Euclid's parallel postulate. _____ are two lines on the same plane that do not intersect even assuming that lines extend to infinity in either direction.
    a. Parallel lines0
    b. Thing
    c. Undefined
    d. Undefined

Chapter 1. Data and Linear representations

49. In mathematics, the multiplicative inverse of a number x, denoted 1/x or x^{-1}, is the number which, when multiplied by x, yields 1. The multiplicative inverse of x is also called the _____ of x.
    a. Thing
    b. Reciprocal0
    c. Undefined
    d. Undefined

50. A _____ is a polygon with four sides and four vertices.
    a. Thing
    b. Quadrilateral0
    c. Undefined
    d. Undefined

51. A _____ is a four-sided plane figure that has two sets of opposite parallel sides.
    a. Parallelogram0
    b. Concept
    c. Undefined
    d. Undefined

52. In geometry, a _____ is defined as a quadrilateral where all four of its angles are right angles.
    a. Rectangle0
    b. Thing
    c. Undefined
    d. Undefined

53. In mathematics, the additive inverse, or _____ of a number n is the number that, when added to n, yields zero. The additive inverse of n is denoted −n. For example, 7 is −7, because 7 + (−7) = 0, and the additive inverse of −0.3 is 0.3, because −0.3 + 0.3 = 0.
    a. Opposite0
    b. Thing
    c. Undefined
    d. Undefined

54. In geometry and trigonometry, a _____ is defined as an angle between two straight intersecting lines of ninety degrees, or one-quarter of a circle.
    a. Right angle0
    b. Thing
    c. Undefined
    d. Undefined

55. _____ is the study of geometry using the principles of algebra. _____ can be explained more simply: it is concerned with defining geometrical shapes in a numerical way and extracting numerical information from that representation.
    a. Thing
    b. Analytic geometry0
    c. Undefined
    d. Undefined

56. In mathematics, the _____ of a number n is the number that, when added to n, yields zero. The _____ of n is denoted −n. For example, 7 is −7, because 7 + (−7) = 0, and the _____ of −0.3 is 0.3, because −0.3 + 0.3 = 0.
    a. Thing
    b. Additive inverse0
    c. Undefined
    d. Undefined

57. In mathematics, the _____ of a function is the set of all "output" values produced by that function. Given a function $f : A \to B$, the _____ of f, is defined to be the set $\{x \in B : x = f(a)$ for some $a \in A\}$.
    a. Thing
    b. Range0
    c. Undefined
    d. Undefined

58. Acid _____ ratio measures the ability of a company to use its near cash or quick assets to immediately extinguish its current liabilities.

Chapter 1. Data and Linear representations

    a. Thing
    b. Test0
    c. Undefined
    d. Undefined

59. In Euclidean geometry, a uniform _____ is a linear transformation that enlargers or diminishes objects, and whose _____ factor is the same in all directions. This is also called homothethy.
    a. Thing
    b. Scale0
    c. Undefined
    d. Undefined

60. _____ is a form of periodic payment from an employer to an employee, which is specified in an employment contract.
    a. Gross pay0
    b. Thing
    c. Undefined
    d. Undefined

61. A _____ is a form of periodic payment from an employer to an employee, which is specified in an employment contract.
    a. Thing
    b. Salary0
    c. Undefined
    d. Undefined

62. The metre (or _____, see spelling differences) is a measure of length. It is the basic unit of length in the metric system and in the International System of Units (SI), used around the world for general and scientific purposes.
    a. Meter0
    b. Concept
    c. Undefined
    d. Undefined

63. The _____ is the distance around a closed curve. _____ is a kind of perimeter.
    a. Circumference0
    b. Thing
    c. Undefined
    d. Undefined

64. In geometry, a _____ (Greek words diairo = divide and metro = measure) of a circle is any straight line segment that passes through the centre and whose endpoints are on the circular boundary, or, in more modern usage, the length of such a line segment. When using the word in the more modern sense, one speaks of the _____ rather than a _____, because all diameters of a circle have the same length. This length is twice the radius. The _____ of a circle is also the longest chord that the circle has.
    a. Diameter0
    b. Thing
    c. Undefined
    d. Undefined

65. _____ are a measure of time.
    a. Minutes0
    b. Thing
    c. Undefined
    d. Undefined

66. _____ is a special mathematical relationship between two quantities. Two quantities are called proportional if they vary in such a way that one of the quantities is a constant multiple of the other, or equivalently if they have a constant ratio.
    a. Proportionality0
    b. Thing
    c. Undefined
    d. Undefined

8 *Chapter 1. Data and Linear representations*

67. In mathematics and logic, a _____ proof is a way of showing the truth or falsehood of a given statement by a straightforward combination of established facts, usually existing lemmas and theorems, without making any further assumptions.
   a. Thing
   b. Direct0
   c. Undefined
   d. Undefined

68. _____ is the relationship between two variables, like a ratio in which the two quantities being compared are different units.
   a. Direct variation0
   b. Thing
   c. Undefined
   d. Undefined

69. A _____ is a negotiable instrument instructing a financial institution to pay a specific amount of a specific currency from a specific demand account held in the maker/depositor's name with that institution. Both the maker and payee may be natural persons or legal entities.
   a. Thing
   b. Check0
   c. Undefined
   d. Undefined

70. In mathematics, two quantities are called _____ if they vary in such a way that one of the quantities is a constant multiple of the other, or equivalently if they have a constant ratio.
   a. Thing
   b. Proportional0
   c. Undefined
   d. Undefined

71. In common philosophical language, a proposition or _____, is the content of an assertion, that is, it is true-or-false and defined by the meaning of a particular piece of language.
   a. Statement0
   b. Concept
   c. Undefined
   d. Undefined

72. _____ (or proportionality) are two quantities that vary in such a way that one of the quatities is a constant multiple of the other, or equivalently if they have a constant ratio.
   a. Thing
   b. Proportions0
   c. Undefined
   d. Undefined

73. The _____, the average in everyday English, which is also called the arithmetic _____ (and is distinguished from the geometric _____ or harmonic _____). The average is also called the sample _____. The expected value of a random variable, which is also called the population _____.
   a. Mean0
   b. Thing
   c. Undefined
   d. Undefined

74. In mathematics, a _____ is the result of multiplying, or an expression that identifies factors to be multiplied.
   a. Thing
   b. Product0
   c. Undefined
   d. Undefined

75. Sir Isaac _____, was an English physicist, mathematician, astronomer, natural philosopher, and alchemist, regarded by many as the greatest figure in the history of science

Chapter 1. Data and Linear representations

    a. Newton0
    b. Person
    c. Undefined
    d. Undefined

76. _____ algebra (sometimes called General algebra) is the field of mathematics that studies the ideas common to all algebraic structures.
    a. Universal0
    b. Thing
    c. Undefined
    d. Undefined

77. A _____, as defined by the International Astronomical Union , is a celestial body orbiting a star or stellar remnant that is massive enough to be rounded by its own gravity, not massive enough to cause thermonuclear fusion in its core, and has cleared its neighboring region of planetesimals.
    a. Planet0
    b. Thing
    c. Undefined
    d. Undefined

78. _____, Greek for "knowledge of nature," is the branch of science concerned with the discovery and characterization of universal laws which govern matter, energy, space, and time.
    a. Thing
    b. Physics0
    c. Undefined
    d. Undefined

79. A _____ is a compensation which workers receive in exchange for their labor.
    a. Thing
    b. Wage0
    c. Undefined
    d. Undefined

80. _____ is the property of a physical object that quantifies the amount of matter and energy it is equivalent to.
    a. Mass0
    b. Thing
    c. Undefined
    d. Undefined

81. A _____ is a unit of length in the metric system, equal to one thousand metres, the current SI base unit of length
    a. Kilometer0
    b. Thing
    c. Undefined
    d. Undefined

82. _____ is the difference of electrical potential between two points of an electrical or electronic circuit, expressed in volts
    a. Voltage0
    b. Thing
    c. Undefined
    d. Undefined

83. The _____, in practice often shortened to amp, is a unit of electric current, or amount of electric charge per second.
    a. Thing
    b. Amperes0
    c. Undefined
    d. Undefined

84. _____ is electromagnetic radiation with a wavelength that is visible to the eye (visible _____) or, in a technical or scientific context, electromagnetic radiation of any wavelength.
    a. Light0
    b. Thing
    c. Undefined
    d. Undefined

Chapter 1. Data and Linear representations

85. _____ is the pressure at some point withig the fluid
   a. Water pressure0
   b. Thing
   c. Undefined
   d. Undefined

86. In mathematics, an inequality is a statement about the relative size or order of two objects. For example 14 > 10, or 14 is _____ 10.
   a. Thing
   b. Greater than0
   c. Undefined
   d. Undefined

87. A _____, scatter diagram or scatter graph is a chart that uses Cartesian coordinates to display values for two variables.
   a. Scatter plot0
   b. Thing
   c. Undefined
   d. Undefined

88. A _____ is a statement or claimt that a particular event will occur in the future in more certain terms than a forecast.
   a. Prediction0
   b. Thing
   c. Undefined
   d. Undefined

89. In probability theory and statistics, _____, also called _____ coefficient, indicates the strength and direction of a linear relationship between two random variables.
   a. Thing
   b. Correlation0
   c. Undefined
   d. Undefined

90. A _____ is a simplified and structured visual representation of concepts, ideas, constructions, relations, statistical data, anatomy etc used in all aspects of human activities to visualize and clarify the topic.
   a. Thing
   b. Diagram0
   c. Undefined
   d. Undefined

91. In mathematics, a _____ is a constant multiplicative factor of a certain object. The object can be such things as a variable, a vector, a function, etc. For example, the _____ of $9x^2$ is 9.
   a. Thing
   b. Coefficient0
   c. Undefined
   d. Undefined

92. In sociology and biology a _____ is the collection of people or organisms of a particular species living in a given geographic area or space, usually measured by a census.
   a. Thing
   b. Population0
   c. Undefined
   d. Undefined

93. _____ is a business term for the amount of money that a company receives from its activities in a given period, mostly from sales of products and/or services to customers
   a. Thing
   b. Revenue0
   c. Undefined
   d. Undefined

94. In mathematics, an _____, mean, or central tendency of a data set refers to a measure of the "middle" or "expected" value of the data set.

a. Average0
b. Concept
c. Undefined
d. Undefined

95. _____ is a graph of the points representing a collection of data.
   a. Thing
   b. Scatter plots0
   c. Undefined
   d. Undefined

96. _____ is a way of expressing a number as a fraction of 100 per cent meaning "per hundred".
   a. Percent0
   b. Thing
   c. Undefined
   d. Undefined

97. An _____ is a combination of numbers, operators, grouping symbols and/or free variables and bound variables arranged in a meaningful way which can be evaluated..
   a. Thing
   b. Expression0
   c. Undefined
   d. Undefined

98. Two mathematical objects are equal if and only if they are precisely the same in every way. This defines a binary relation, _____, denoted by the sign of _____ "=" in such a way that the statement "x = y" means that x and y are equal.
   a. Thing
   b. Equality0
   c. Undefined
   d. Undefined

99. In mathematics, _____ is an elementary arithmetic operation. When one of the numbers is a whole number, _____ is the repeated sum of the other number.
   a. Thing
   b. Multiplication0
   c. Undefined
   d. Undefined

100. _____ is a fixed, but possibly unspecified, value. This is in contrast to a variable, which is not fixed.
   a. Constant term0
   b. Thing
   c. Undefined
   d. Undefined

101. _____, either of the curved-bracket punctuation marks that together make a set of _____
   a. Parentheses0
   b. Thing
   c. Undefined
   d. Undefined

102. In mathematics, the _____ of two sets A and B is the set that contains all elements of A that also belong to B (or equivalently, all elements of B that also belong to A), but no other elements.
   a. Thing
   b. Intersection0
   c. Undefined
   d. Undefined

103. The _____ is a property of multiplication or addition where the product or sum remains the same, regardless of whether or not the order of the addends or factors are changed.
   a. Commutative property0
   b. Thing
   c. Undefined
   d. Undefined

104. A pair of angles is _____ if their respective measures sum to 180 degrees.

Chapter 1. Data and Linear representations

a. Concept
b. Supplementary0
c. Undefined
d. Undefined

105. A _____ is a function that assigns a number to subsets of a given set.
a. Measure0
b. Thing
c. Undefined
d. Undefined

106. In classical geometry, a _____ of a circle or sphere is any line segment from its center to its boundary. By extension, the _____ of a circle or sphere is the length of any such segment. The _____ is half the diameter. In science and engineering the term _____ of curvature is commonly used as a synonym for _____.
a. Thing
b. Radius0
c. Undefined
d. Undefined

107. The _____ of a right circular cone is the distance from any point on the circle to the apex of the cone.
a. Thing
b. Slant height0
c. Undefined
d. Undefined

108. A _____ is a three-dimensional geometric shape formed by straight lines through a fixed point (vertex) to the points of a fixed curve (directrix)
a. Cone0
b. Concept
c. Undefined
d. Undefined

109. A _____ is a type of debt. All material things can be lent but this article focuses exclusively on monetary loans. Like all debt instruments, a _____ entails the redistribution of financial assets over time, between the lender and the borrower.
a. Loan0
b. Thing
c. Undefined
d. Undefined

110. Mathematical _____ is used to represent ideas.
a. Notation0
b. Thing
c. Undefined
d. Undefined

111. _____ is the writing of numbers in the base-ten numeral system, which uses various symbols called digits for ten distinct values 0, 1, 2, 3, 4, 5, 6, 7, 8 and 9 to represent numbers
a. Thing
b. Decimal notation0
c. Undefined
d. Undefined

112. _____ is a notation for writing numbers that is often used by scientists and mathematicians to make it easier to write large and small numbers.
a. Thing
b. Scientific notation0
c. Undefined
d. Undefined

113. Kepler's laws of _____ are his primary contributions to astronomy/astrophysics. Kepler, a German mathematician, studied the observations of the legendarily precise Danish astronomer Tycho Brahe, and found around 1605 that these observations followed three relatively simple mathematical laws.

Chapter 1. Data and Linear representations

a. Planetary motion0
b. Thing
c. Undefined
d. Undefined

114. A _____ is a deliberate process for transforming one or more inputs into one or more results.
   a. Thing
   b. Calculation0
   c. Undefined
   d. Undefined

115. In mathematics, an _____ is a statement about the relative size or order of two objects.
   a. Inequality0
   b. Thing
   c. Undefined
   d. Undefined

116. _____ interest refers to the fact that whenever interest is calculated, it is based not only on the original principal, but also on any unpaid interest that has been added to the principal.
   a. Compound0
   b. Thing
   c. Undefined
   d. Undefined

117. In mathematics, _____ geometry was the traditional name for the geometry of three-dimensional Euclidean space — for practical purposes the kind of space we live in.
   a. Thing
   b. Solid0
   c. Undefined
   d. Undefined

118. _____ forms part of thinking. Considered the most complex of all intellectual functions, _____ has been defined as higher-order cognitive process that requires the modulation and control of more routine or fundamental skills.
   a. Problem solving0
   b. Thing
   c. Undefined
   d. Undefined

119. A _____ is a one-dimensional picture in which the integers are shown as specially-marked points evenly spaced on a line.
   a. Thing
   b. Number line0
   c. Undefined
   d. Undefined

120. _____ is the level of functional and/or metabolic efficiency of an organism at both the micro level.
   a. Health0
   b. Thing
   c. Undefined
   d. Undefined

121. _____, from Latin meaning "to make progress", is defined in two different ways. Pure economic _____ is the increase in wealth that an investor has from making an investment, taking into consideration all costs associated with that investment including the opportunity cost of capital.
   a. Thing
   b. Profit0
   c. Undefined
   d. Undefined

122. _____ are citizens in a democratic form of governance that have checked in with some form of a central registry, which in turn permits them to vote.
   a. Thing
   b. Registered voters0
   c. Undefined
   d. Undefined

Chapter 1. Data and Linear representations

123. _____ finance, in finance, a debt security, issued by Issuer
- a. Bond0
- b. Thing
- c. Undefined
- d. Undefined

124. _____ is a subset of a population.
- a. Thing
- b. Sample0
- c. Undefined
- d. Undefined

125. _____ is the application of tools and a processing medium to the transformation of raw materials into finished goods for sale.
- a. Thing
- b. Manufacturing0
- c. Undefined
- d. Undefined

126. In mathematics, the _____ (or modulus) of a real number is its numerical value without regard to its sign.
- a. Absolute value0
- b. Thing
- c. Undefined
- d. Undefined

127. The _____ integers are all the integers from zero on upwards.
- a. Nonnegative0
- b. Thing
- c. Undefined
- d. Undefined

128. _____ is a general method of problem solving for obtaining knowledge, both propositional and know-how. It is used typically in elementary algebra, when solving equations.
- a. Thing
- b. Guess and check0
- c. Undefined
- d. Undefined

129. _____ is the estimation of a physical quantity such as distance, energy, temperature, or time.
- a. Measurement0
- b. Thing
- c. Undefined
- d. Undefined

130. _____ is a term applied when talking about the movement of air from one place to the next.
- a. Thing
- b. Wind speed0
- c. Undefined
- d. Undefined

131. _____ are activities that are governed by a set of rules or customs and often engaged in competitively.
- a. Thing
- b. Sports0
- c. Undefined
- d. Undefined

132. In mathematics, a _____ number is a number which can be expressed as a ratio of two integers. Non-integer _____ numbers (commonly called fractions) are usually written as the vulgar fraction a / b, where b is not zero.
- a. Thing
- b. Rational0
- c. Undefined
- d. Undefined

133. _____ consists either of a suggested explanation for a phenomenon or of a reasoned proposal suggesting a possible correlation between multiple phenomena.

Chapter 1. Data and Linear representations

    a. Hypotheses0   b. Event
    c. Undefined   d. Undefined

134. _____ is a mathematical science pertaining to the collection, analysis, interpretation or explanation, and presentation of data. It is applicable to a wide variety of academic disciplines, from the physical and social sciences to the humanities.
    a. Statistics0   b. Thing
    c. Undefined   d. Undefined

135. An _____ or bill is a commercial document issued by a seller to a buyer, indicating the products, quantities and agreed prices for products or services with which the seller has already provided the buyer.
    a. Invoice0   b. Thing
    c. Undefined   d. Undefined

136. A _____ is one of the basic shapes of geometry: a polygon with three vertices and three sides which are straight line segments.
    a. Triangle0   b. Thing
    c. Undefined   d. Undefined

137. The _____ of a right triangle is the triangle's longest side; the side opposite the right angle.
    a. Hypotenuse0   b. Thing
    c. Undefined   d. Undefined

138. _____ studies and addresses the ways in which individuals, businesses, and organizations raise, allocate, and use monetary resources over time, taking into account the risks entailed in their projects
    a. Finance0   b. Thing
    c. Undefined   d. Undefined

139. A _____ fraction is a fraction in which the absolute value of the numerator is less than the denominator--hence, the absolute value of the fraction is less than 1.
    a. Thing   b. Proper0
    c. Undefined   d. Undefined

140. The _____ , is named after Alexander Henry Rhind, a Scottish antiquarian, who purchased the papyrus in 1858 in Luxor, Egypt; it was apparently found during illegal excavations in or near the Ramesseum.
    a. Thing   b. Rhind papyrus0
    c. Undefined   d. Undefined

141. Mathematical _____ are the wide variety of ways to capture an abstract mathematical concept or relationship.
    a. Thing   b. Representations0
    c. Undefined   d. Undefined

142. In linear algebra, the _____ of an n-by-n square matrix A is defined to be the sum of the elements on the main diagonal of A,

Chapter 1. Data and Linear representations

a. Trace0
b. Thing
c. Undefined
d. Undefined

143. In mathematics, a _____ is an ordered list of objects. Like a set, it contains members, also called elements or terms, and the number of terms is called the length of the _____. Unlike a set, order matters, and the exact same elements can appear multiple times at different positions in the _____.

a. Sequence0
b. Thing
c. Undefined
d. Undefined

144. The _____ or kilogramme is the SI base unit of mass. It is defined as being equal to the mass of the international prototype of the _____.

a. Kilogram0
b. Thing
c. Undefined
d. Undefined

145. A _____ is an abstract model that uses mathematical language to describe the behavior of a system. Eykhoff defined a _____ as 'a representation of the essential aspects of an existing system which presents knowledge of that system in usable form'.

a. Mathematical model0
b. Thing
c. Undefined
d. Undefined

146. _____ is a set, with some particular properties and usually some additional structure, such as the operations of addition or multiplication, for instance.

a. Thing
b. Space0
c. Undefined
d. Undefined

Chapter 2. Numbers and Functions

1. In arithmetic and algebra, when a number or expression is both preceded and followed by a binary operation, an _____ is required for which operation should be applied first.
   a. Order of operations0
   b. Thing
   c. Undefined
   d. Undefined

2. An _____ is a combination of numbers, operators, grouping symbols and/or free variables and bound variables arranged in a meaningful way which can be evaluated..
   a. Thing
   b. Expression0
   c. Undefined
   d. Undefined

3. In mathematics, a _____ number is a number which can be expressed as a ratio of two integers. Non-integer _____ numbers (commonly called fractions) are usually written as the vulgar fraction a / b, where b is not zero.
   a. Thing
   b. Rational0
   c. Undefined
   d. Undefined

4. _____ is a physical property of a system that underlies the common notions of hot and cold; something that is hotter has the greater _____.
   a. Thing
   b. Temperature0
   c. Undefined
   d. Undefined

5. _____ is the interdisciplinary scientific study of the atmosphere that focuses on weather processes and forecasting.
   a. Meteorology0
   b. Thing
   c. Undefined
   d. Undefined

6. A _____ decimal is a number whose decimal representation eventually becomes periodic (i.e. the same number sequence _____ indefinitely).
   a. Repeating0
   b. Thing
   c. Undefined
   d. Undefined

7. A _____ decimal is a decimal fraction which ends after a definite number of digits.
   a. Thing
   b. Terminating0
   c. Undefined
   d. Undefined

8. The _____ (symbol _____) and the millibar (symbol mbar, also mb) are units of pressure.
   a. Thing
   b. Bar0
   c. Undefined
   d. Undefined

9. In mathematics, a _____ may be described informally as a number that can be given by an infinite decimal representation.
   a. Real number0
   b. Thing
   c. Undefined
   d. Undefined

10. In mathematics, _____ is an elementary arithmetic operation. When one of the numbers is a whole number, _____ is the repeated sum of the other number.

Chapter 2. Numbers and Functions

    a. Thing
    b. Multiplication0
    c. Undefined
    d. Undefined

11. In mathematics, and in particular in abstract algebra, the _____ is a property of binary operations that generalises the distributive law from elementary algebra.
    a. Distributive property0
    b. Thing
    c. Undefined
    d. Undefined

12. The _____ is a property of multiplication or addition where the product or sum remains the same, regardless of whether or not the order of the addends or factors are changed.
    a. Thing
    b. Commutative property0
    c. Undefined
    d. Undefined

13. A _____ is a consumption tax charged at the point of purchase for certain goods and services.
    a. Thing
    b. Sales tax0
    c. Undefined
    d. Undefined

14. In abstract algebra, _____ consists of sets with binary operations that satisfy certain axioms.
    a. Thing
    b. Grouping0
    c. Undefined
    d. Undefined

15. _____ are objects, characters, or other concrete representations of ideas, concepts, or other abstractions.
    a. Thing
    b. Symbols0
    c. Undefined
    d. Undefined

16. _____ is a mathematical operation, written a^n, involving two numbers, the base a and the exponent n.
    a. Exponentiating0
    b. Thing
    c. Undefined
    d. Undefined

17. _____ is a mathematical operation, written a^n, involving two numbers, the base a and the exponent n.
    a. Thing
    b. Exponentiation0
    c. Undefined
    d. Undefined

18. _____ has many meanings, most of which simply .
    a. Power0
    b. Thing
    c. Undefined
    d. Undefined

19. A _____ is a numeral used to indicate a count. The most common use of the word today is to name the part of a fraction that tells the number or count of equal parts.
    a. Numerator0
    b. Thing
    c. Undefined
    d. Undefined

20. _____, either of the curved-bracket punctuation marks that together make a set of _____.
    a. Parentheses0
    b. Thing
    c. Undefined
    d. Undefined

Chapter 2. Numbers and Functions

21. _____ is often used to describe the measurement of the steepness, incline, gradient, or grade of a straight line. The _____ is defined as the ratio of the "rise" divided by the "run" between two points on a line, or in other words, the ratio of the altitude change to the horizontal distance between any two points on the line.
    a. Thing
    b. Slope0
    c. Undefined
    d. Undefined

22. A _____ is the part of a fraction that tells how many equal parts make up a whole, and which is used in the name of the fraction: "halves", "thirds", "fourths" or "quarters", "fifths" and so on.
    a. Denominator0
    b. Concept
    c. Undefined
    d. Undefined

23. _____, in law and economics, is a form of risk management primarily used to hedge against the risk of a contingent loss.
    a. Thing
    b. Insurance0
    c. Undefined
    d. Undefined

24. A _____ is a one-dimensional picture in which the integers are shown as specially-marked points evenly spaced on a line.
    a. Number line0
    b. Thing
    c. Undefined
    d. Undefined

25. _____ is a mathematical science pertaining to the collection, analysis, interpretation or explanation, and presentation of data. It is applicable to a wide variety of academic disciplines, from the physical and social sciences to the humanities.
    a. Statistics0
    b. Thing
    c. Undefined
    d. Undefined

26. In mathematics, an _____, mean, or central tendency of a data set refers to a measure of the "middle" or "expected" value of the data set.
    a. Average0
    b. Concept
    c. Undefined
    d. Undefined

27. A _____ was a citizen of Babylonia, named for its capital city, Babylon, which was an ancient state in the south part of Mesopotamia (in modern Iraq), combining the territories of Sumer and Akkad.
    a. Babylonian0
    b. Place
    c. Undefined
    d. Undefined

28. In mathematics, an _____ number is any real number that is not a rational number- that is, it is a number which cannot be expressed as a fraction m/n, where m and n are integers.
    a. Irrational0
    b. Thing
    c. Undefined
    d. Undefined

29. In mathematics, an _____ is any real number that is not a rational number ¡ª that is, it is a number which cannot be expressed as m/n, where m and n are integers.

a. Thing
b. Irrational number0
c. Undefined
d. Undefined

30. In mathematics, _____ are any real number that is not a rational number ¡ª that is, it is a number which cannot be expressed as m/n, where m and n are integers.
   a. Irrational numbers0
   b. Thing
   c. Undefined
   d. Undefined

31. In plane geometry, a _____ is a polygon with four equal sides, four right angles, and parallel opposite sides. In algebra, the _____ of a number is that number multiplied by itself.
   a. Thing
   b. Square0
   c. Undefined
   d. Undefined

32. _____ is the level of functional and/or metabolic efficiency of an organism at both the micro level.
   a. Health0
   b. Thing
   c. Undefined
   d. Undefined

33. A _____ is a deliberate process for transforming one or more inputs into one or more results.
   a. Calculation0
   b. Thing
   c. Undefined
   d. Undefined

34. _____ is a type of insurance whereby the insurer pays the medical costs of the insured if the insured becomes sick due to covered causes, or due to accidents.
   a. Thing
   b. Medical insurance0
   c. Undefined
   d. Undefined

35. _____ refers to selected population characteristics as used in government, marketing or opinion research, or the demographic profiles used in such research.
   a. Demographics0
   b. Thing
   c. Undefined
   d. Undefined

36. In mathematics, an _____ is a statement about the relative size or order of two objects.
   a. Thing
   b. Inequality0
   c. Undefined
   d. Undefined

37. A _____ is a number that is less than zero.
   a. Thing
   b. Negative number0
   c. Undefined
   d. Undefined

38. The _____ integers are all the integers from zero on upwards.
   a. Nonnegative0
   b. Thing
   c. Undefined
   d. Undefined

39. _____ is a set, with some particular properties and usually some additional structure, such as the operations of addition or multiplication, for instance.

Chapter 2. Numbers and Functions

a. Space0
b. Thing
c. Undefined
d. Undefined

40. In physics, an _____ is the path that an object makes around another object while under the influence of a source of centripetal force, such as gravity.
    a. Orbit0
    b. Thing
    c. Undefined
    d. Undefined

41. In physics, _____ is an influence that may cause an object to accelerate. It may be experienced as a lift, a push, or a pull. The actual acceleration of the body is determined by the vector sum of all forces acting on it, known as net _____ or resultant _____.
    a. Thing
    b. Force0
    c. Undefined
    d. Undefined

42. A _____ is a special kind of ratio, indicating a relationship between two measurements with different units, such as miles to gallons or cents to pounds.
    a. Thing
    b. Rate0
    c. Undefined
    d. Undefined

43. In mathematics, a _____ can mean either an element of the set {1, 2, 3, ...} (i.e the positive integers) or an element of the set {0, 1, 2, 3, ...} (i.e. the non-negative integers).
    a. Whole number0
    b. Concept
    c. Undefined
    d. Undefined

44. _____ is the transport of people on a trip/journey or the process or time involved in a person or object moving from one location to another.
    a. Thing
    b. Travel0
    c. Undefined
    d. Undefined

45. In Euclidean geometry, a _____ is the set of all points in a plane at a fixed distance, called the radius, from a given point, the center.
    a. Circle0
    b. Thing
    c. Undefined
    d. Undefined

46. _____ is defined as the rate of change or derivative with respect to time of velocity.
    a. Acceleration0
    b. Thing
    c. Undefined
    d. Undefined

47. In mathematics, a _____ can mean either an element of the set {1, 2, 3, ...} (i.e the positive integers or the counting numbers) or an element of the set {0, 1, 2, 3, ...} (i.e. the non-negative integers).
    a. Thing
    b. Natural number0
    c. Undefined
    d. Undefined

48. In mathematics, defined and _____ are used to explain whether or not expressions have meaningful, sensible, and unambiguous values.

a. Thing
b. Undefined0
c. Undefined
d. Undefined

49. In mathematics, _____ expressions is used to reduce the expression into the lowest possible term.
   a. Simplifying0
   b. Thing
   c. Undefined
   d. Undefined

50. _____ is the mathematical action of repeatedly adding or subtracting one, usually to find out how many objects there are or to set aside a desired number of objects.
   a. Counting0
   b. Thing
   c. Undefined
   d. Undefined

51. In mathematics, factorization (British English: factorisation) or factoring is the decomposition of an object (for example, a number, a polynomial, or a matrix) into a product of other objects, or _____, which when multiplied together give the original.
   a. Thing
   b. Factors0
   c. Undefined
   d. Undefined

52. A _____ is a symbolic representation denoting a quantity or expression. It often represents an "unknown" quantity that has the potential to change.
   a. Thing
   b. Variable0
   c. Undefined
   d. Undefined

53. In mathematics, a _____ is the result of multiplying, or an expression that identifies factors to be multiplied.
   a. Product0
   b. Thing
   c. Undefined
   d. Undefined

54. The _____ are the only integral domain whose positive elements are well-ordered, and in which order is preserved by addition. Like the natural numbers, the _____ form a countably infinite set. The set of all _____ is usually denoted in mathematics by a boldface Z .
   a. Integers0
   b. Thing
   c. Undefined
   d. Undefined

55. A _____ is a negotiable instrument instructing a financial institution to pay a specific amount of a specific currency from a specific demand account held in the maker/depositor's name with that institution. Both the maker and payee may be natural persons or legal entities.
   a. Thing
   b. Check0
   c. Undefined
   d. Undefined

56. The metre (or _____, see spelling differences) is a measure of length. It is the basic unit of length in the metric system and in the International System of Units (SI), used around the world for general and scientific purposes.
   a. Meter0
   b. Concept
   c. Undefined
   d. Undefined

57. The _____ or kilogramme is the SI base unit of mass. It is defined as being equal to the mass of the international prototype of the _____.

Chapter 2. Numbers and Functions

a. Kilogram0
b. Thing
c. Undefined
d. Undefined

58. Equivalence is the condition of being _____ or essentially equal.
    a. Thing
    b. Equivalent0
    c. Undefined
    d. Undefined

59. In classical geometry, a _____ of a circle or sphere is any line segment from its center to its boundary. By extension, the _____ of a circle or sphere is the length of any such segment. The _____ is half the diameter. In science and engineering the term _____ of curvature is commonly used as a synonym for _____.
    a. Thing
    b. Radius0
    c. Undefined
    d. Undefined

60. _____, Greek for "knowledge of nature," is the branch of science concerned with the discovery and characterization of universal laws which govern matter, energy, space, and time.
    a. Thing
    b. Physics0
    c. Undefined
    d. Undefined

61. A _____ is a movement of an object in a circular motion. A two-dimensional object rotates around a center (or point) of _____. A three-dimensional object rotates around a line called an axis. If the axis of _____ is within the body, the body is said to rotate upon itself, or spinâ€"which implies relative speed and perhaps free-movement with angular momentum. A circular motion about an external point, e.g. the Earth about the Sun, is called an orbit or more properly an orbital revolution.
    a. Rotation0
    b. Thing
    c. Undefined
    d. Undefined

62. The _____ of a solid object is the three-dimensional concept of how much space it occupies, often quantified numerically.
    a. Volume0
    b. Thing
    c. Undefined
    d. Undefined

63. _____ is a three-dimensional geometric shape formed by straight lines through a fixed point vertex to the points of a fixed curve directrix.
    a. Thing
    b. Right circular cone0
    c. Undefined
    d. Undefined

64. A _____ is a three-dimensional geometric shape formed by straight lines through a fixed point (vertex) to the points of a fixed curve (directrix)
    a. Cone0
    b. Concept
    c. Undefined
    d. Undefined

65. _____ is the design, analysis, and/or construction of works for practical purposes.
    a. Thing
    b. Engineering0
    c. Undefined
    d. Undefined

Chapter 2. Numbers and Functions

66. In mathematics, a matrix can be thought of as each row or _____ being a vector. Hence, a space formed by row vectors or _____ vectors are said to be a row space or a _____ space.
   a. Column0
   b. Concept
   c. Undefined
   d. Undefined

67. In geometry, a _____ (Greek words diairo = divide and metro = measure) of a circle is any straight line segment that passes through the centre and whose endpoints are on the circular boundary, or, in more modern usage, the length of such a line segment. When using the word in the more modern sense, one speaks of the _____ rather than a _____, because all diameters of a circle have the same length. This length is twice the radius. The _____ of a circle is also the longest chord that the circle has.
   a. Thing
   b. Diameter0
   c. Undefined
   d. Undefined

68. _____ is the force that opposes the relative motion or tendency toward such motion of two surfaces in contact.
   a. Thing
   b. Friction0
   c. Undefined
   d. Undefined

69. _____ is a way of expressing a number as a fraction of 100 per cent meaning "per hundred".
   a. Percent0
   b. Thing
   c. Undefined
   d. Undefined

70. In geometry, an _____ of a triangle is a straight line through a vertex and perpendicular to (i.e. forming a right angle with) the opposite side or an extension of the opposite side.
   a. Altitude0
   b. Concept
   c. Undefined
   d. Undefined

71. The State of _____ is a state located in the Rocky Mountain region of the United States of America.
   a. Thing
   b. Colorado0
   c. Undefined
   d. Undefined

72. A _____ is a unit of length, usually used to measure distance, in a number of different systems, including Imperial units, United States customary units and Norwegian/Swedish mil. Its size can vary from system to system, but in each is between 1 and 10 kilometers. In contemporary English contexts _____ refers to either:
   a. Thing
   b. Mile0
   c. Undefined
   d. Undefined

73. _____ is a state located in the southern and southwestern regions of the United States of America.
   a. Texas0
   b. Thing
   c. Undefined
   d. Undefined

74. In mathematics, the _____ of a function is the set of all "output" values produced by that function. Given a function $f: A \to B$, the _____ of f, is defined to be the set $\{x \in B : x = f(a) \text{ for some } a \in A\}$.
   a. Thing
   b. Range0
   c. Undefined
   d. Undefined

Chapter 2. Numbers and Functions

75. The mathematical concept of a _____ expresses the intuitive idea of deterministic dependence between two quantities, one of which is viewed as primary and the other as secondary. A _____ then is a way to associate a unique output for each input of a specified type, for example, a real number or an element of a given set.
   a. Thing
   b. Function0
   c. Undefined
   d. Undefined

76. In mathematics, a _____ of a k-place relation $L \subseteq X_1 \times \ldots \times X_k$ is one of the sets X_j, $1 \leq j \leq k$. In the special case where k = 2 and $L \subseteq X_1 \times X_2$ is a function $L : X_1 \to X_2$, it is conventional to refer to X_1 as the _____ of the function and to refer to X_2 as the codomain of the function.
   a. Domain0
   b. Thing
   c. Undefined
   d. Undefined

77. Mathematical _____ is used to represent ideas.
   a. Notation0
   b. Thing
   c. Undefined
   d. Undefined

78. _____ is the distance around a given two-dimensional object. As a general rule, the _____ of a polygon can always be calculated by adding all the length of the sides together. So, the formula for triangles is P = a + b + c, where a, b and c stand for each side of it. For quadrilaterals the equation is P = a + b + c + d. For equilateral polygons, P = na, where n is the number of sides and a is the side length.
   a. Thing
   b. Perimeter0
   c. Undefined
   d. Undefined

79. Acid _____ ratio measures the ability of a company to use its near cash or quick assets to immediately extinguish its current liabilities.
   a. Test0
   b. Thing
   c. Undefined
   d. Undefined

80. _____ are a measure of time.
   a. Minutes0
   b. Thing
   c. Undefined
   d. Undefined

81. U.S. liquid _____ is legally defined as 231 cubic inches, and is equal to 3.785411784 litres or abotu 0.13368 cubic feet. This is the most common definition of a _____. The U.S. fluid ounce is defined as 1/128 of a U.S. _____.
   a. Gallon0
   b. Thing
   c. Undefined
   d. Undefined

82. A _____ are accounts maintained by commercial banks, savings and loan associations, credit unions, and mutual savings banks that pay interest but can not be used directly as money by, for example, writing a cheque.
   a. Thing
   b. Savings account0
   c. Undefined
   d. Undefined

83. An _____ is a collection of two not necessarily distinct objects, one of which is distinguished as the first coordinate and the other as the second coordinate.

Chapter 2. Numbers and Functions

    a. Thing
    b. Ordered pair0
    c. Undefined
    d. Undefined

84. In mathematics, the conjugate _____ or adjoint matrix of an m-by-n matrix A with complex entries is the n-by-m matrix A* obtained from A by taking the transpose and then taking the complex conjugate of each entry.
    a. Pairs0
    b. Thing
    c. Undefined
    d. Undefined

85. The word _____ comes from the 15th Century Latin word discretus which means separate.
    a. Thing
    b. Discrete0
    c. Undefined
    d. Undefined

86. In geometry, a line _____ is a part of a line that is bounded by two end points, and contains every point on the line between its end points.
    a. Segment0
    b. Concept
    c. Undefined
    d. Undefined

87. A _____ function is a function for which, intuitively, small changes in the input result in small changes in the output.
    a. Continuous0
    b. Event
    c. Undefined
    d. Undefined

88. A _____ given two distinct points A and B on the _____, is the set of points C on the line containing points A and B such that A is not strictly between C and B.
    a. Ray0
    b. Thing
    c. Undefined
    d. Undefined

89. In mathematics, the concept of a _____ tries to capture the intuitive idea of a geometrical one-dimensional and continuous object. A simple example is the circle.
    a. Curve0
    b. Thing
    c. Undefined
    d. Undefined

90. In mathematics, an _____ is any of the arguments, i.e. "inputs", to a function. Thus if we have a function $f(x)$, then x is a _____.
    a. Independent variable0
    b. Thing
    c. Undefined
    d. Undefined

91. In a function the _____, is the variable which is the value, i.e. the "output", of the function.
    a. Dependent variable0
    b. Thing
    c. Undefined
    d. Undefined

92. The word _____ comes from the Latin word linearis, which means created by lines.
    a. Thing
    b. Linear0
    c. Undefined
    d. Undefined

Chapter 2. Numbers and Functions

93. A _____ is a first degree polynomial mathematical function of the form: f(x) = mx + b where m and b are real constants and x is a real variable.
    a. Linear function0
    b. Thing
    c. Undefined
    d. Undefined

94. The deductive-nomological model is a formalized view of scientific _____ in natural language.
    a. Thing
    b. Explanation0
    c. Undefined
    d. Undefined

95. _____ is a kind of property which exists as magnitude or multitude. It is among the basic classes of things along with quality, substance, change, and relation.
    a. Amount0
    b. Thing
    c. Undefined
    d. Undefined

96. A _____ is a three-dimensional solid object bounded by six square faces, facets, or sides, with three meeting at each vertex.
    a. Thing
    b. Cube0
    c. Undefined
    d. Undefined

97. A _____ is an individual or household that purchases and uses goods and services generated within the economy.
    a. Thing
    b. Consumer0
    c. Undefined
    d. Undefined

98. In geometry, two lines or planes if one falls on the other in such a way as to create congruent adjacent angles. The term may be used as a noun or adjective. Thus, referring to Figure 1, the line AB is the _____ to CD through the point B.
    a. Thing
    b. Perpendicular0
    c. Undefined
    d. Undefined

99. _____ is a synonym for information.
    a. Data0
    b. Thing
    c. Undefined
    d. Undefined

100. In geographic information systems, a _____ comprises an entity with a geographic location, typically determined by points, arcs, or polygons. Carriageways and cadastres exemplify _____ data.
    a. Feature0
    b. Thing
    c. Undefined
    d. Undefined

101. _____ is a regression method that models the relationship between a dependent variable Y, independent variables Xp, and a random term å.
    a. Thing
    b. Linear regression0
    c. Undefined
    d. Undefined

102. In mathematics, _____ growth occurs when the growth rate of a function is always proportional to the function's current size.

Chapter 2. Numbers and Functions

    a. Thing
    b. Exponential0
    c. Undefined
    d. Undefined

103. A _____, scatter diagram or scatter graph is a chart that uses Cartesian coordinates to display values for two variables.
    a. Scatter plot0
    b. Thing
    c. Undefined
    d. Undefined

104. A _____ is a statement or claimt that a particular event will occur in the future in more certain terms than a forecast.
    a. Thing
    b. Prediction0
    c. Undefined
    d. Undefined

105. Transport or _____ is the movement of people and goods from one place to another.
    a. Thing
    b. Transportation0
    c. Undefined
    d. Undefined

106. _____ is a unit of speed, expressing the number of international miles covered per hour.
    a. Miles per hour0
    b. Thing
    c. Undefined
    d. Undefined

107. A _____ is the result of the addition of a set of numbers. The numbers may be natural numbers, complex numbers, matrices, or still more complicated objects. An infinite _____ is a subtle procedure known as a series.
    a. Thing
    b. Sum0
    c. Undefined
    d. Undefined

108. In mathematics, a _____ of a positive integer n is a way of writing n as a sum of positive integers.
    a. Thing
    b. Composition0
    c. Undefined
    d. Undefined

109. A _____ number is a positive integer which has a positive divisor other than one or itself.
    a. Composite0
    b. Thing
    c. Undefined
    d. Undefined

110. A _____, formed by the composition of one function on another, represents the application of the former to the result of the application of the latter to the argument of the composite.
    a. Thing
    b. Composite function0
    c. Undefined
    d. Undefined

111. The _____ functions is determined by the nesting of two or more functions to form a single new function.
    a. Composition of two0
    b. Thing
    c. Undefined
    d. Undefined

112. In geometry, the _____ of an object is a point in some sense in the middle of the object.

a. Center0
c. Undefined
b. Thing
d. Undefined

113. _____ is a temperature scale named after the German physicist Daniel Gabriel _____ , who proposed it in 1724.
   a. Thing
   b. Fahrenheit0
   c. Undefined
   d. Undefined

114. _____ is, or relates to, the _____ temperature scale .
   a. Thing
   b. Celsius0
   c. Undefined
   d. Undefined

115. In mathematics, there are several meanings of _____ depending on the subject.
   a. Degree0
   b. Thing
   c. Undefined
   d. Undefined

116. The plus and _____ signs are mathematical symbols used to represent the notions of positive and negative as well as the operations of addition and subtraction.
   a. Minus0
   b. Thing
   c. Undefined
   d. Undefined

117. In finance and economics, _____ is the process of finding the present value of an amount of cash at some future date, and along with compounding cash forms the basis of time value of money calculations.
   a. Thing
   b. Discount0
   c. Undefined
   d. Undefined

118. In probability theory and statistics, _____, also called _____ coefficient, indicates the strength and direction of a linear relationship between two random variables.
   a. Thing
   b. Correlation0
   c. Undefined
   d. Undefined

119. In mathematics, a _____ is a constant multiplicative factor of a certain object. The object can be such things as a variable, a vector, a function, etc. For example, the _____ of $9x^2$ is 9.
   a. Coefficient0
   b. Thing
   c. Undefined
   d. Undefined

120. In mathematics, in the field of group theory, a _____ of a group is a quasisimple subnormal subgroup.
   a. Concept
   b. Component0
   c. Undefined
   d. Undefined

121. _____ element of an element x with respect to a binary operation * with identity element e is an element y such that x * y = y * x = e. In particular,
   a. Thing
   b. Inverse0
   c. Undefined
   d. Undefined

Chapter 2. Numbers and Functions

122. In mathematics, the _____ f is the collection of all ordered pairs . In particular, graph means the graphical representation of this collection, in the form of a curve or surface, together with axes, etc. Graphing on a Cartesian plane is sometimes referred to as curve sketching.
    a. Thing
    b. Graph of a function0
    c. Undefined
    d. Undefined

123. In mathematics, a _____ (also spelled reflexion) is a map that transforms an object into its mirror image.
    a. Concept
    b. Reflection0
    c. Undefined
    d. Undefined

124. In mathematics, _____ is a part of the set theoretic notion of function.
    a. Image0
    b. Thing
    c. Undefined
    d. Undefined

125. In astronomy, geography, geometry and related sciences and contexts, a plane is said to be _____ at a given point if it is locally perpendicular to the gradient of the gravity field, i.e., with the direction of the gravitational force at that point.
    a. Horizontal0
    b. Thing
    c. Undefined
    d. Undefined

126. _____ are the basic objects of study in graph theory. Informally speaking, a graph is a set of objects called points, nodes, or vertices connected by links called lines or edges.
    a. Graphs0
    b. Thing
    c. Undefined
    d. Undefined

127. An _____ is an equality that remains true regardless of the values of any variables that appear within it, to distinguish it from an equality which is true under more particular conditions.
    a. Identity0
    b. Thing
    c. Undefined
    d. Undefined

128. An _____ is a function that does not have any effect: it always returns the same value that was used as its argument.
    a. Identity function0
    b. Thing
    c. Undefined
    d. Undefined

129. The _____, the average in everyday English, which is also called the arithmetic _____ (and is distinguished from the geometric _____ or harmonic _____). The average is also called the sample _____. The expected value of a random variable, which is also called the population _____.
    a. Thing
    b. Mean0
    c. Undefined
    d. Undefined

130. In Euclidean geometry, a uniform _____ is a linear transformation that enlargers or diminishes objects, and whose _____ factor is the same in all directions. This is also called homothethy.
    a. Thing
    b. Scale0
    c. Undefined
    d. Undefined

Chapter 2. Numbers and Functions

131. _____ is a business term for the amount of money that a company receives from its activities in a given period, mostly from sales of products and/or services to customers
   a. Thing
   b. Revenue0
   c. Undefined
   d. Undefined

132. A _____ defined function f(x) of a real variable x is a function whose definition is given differently on disjoint subsets of its domain.
   a. Piecewise0
   b. Thing
   c. Undefined
   d. Undefined

133. In mathematics, the _____ (or modulus) of a real number is its numerical value without regard to its sign.
   a. Thing
   b. Absolute value0
   c. Undefined
   d. Undefined

134. A _____ is a compensation which workers receive in exchange for their labor.
   a. Wage0
   b. Thing
   c. Undefined
   d. Undefined

135. A function on the real numbers is called a _____ if it can be written as a finite linear combination of indicator functions of half-open intervals.
   a. Thing
   b. Step function0
   c. Undefined
   d. Undefined

136. In mathematics and the mathematical sciences, a _____ is a fixed, but possibly unspecified, value. This is in contrast to a variable, which is not fixed.
   a. Constant0
   b. Thing
   c. Undefined
   d. Undefined

137. In elementary algebra, an _____ is a set that contains every real number between two indicated numbers and may contain the two numbers themselves.
   a. Interval0
   b. Thing
   c. Undefined
   d. Undefined

138. _____ is the process of reducing the number of significant digits in a number.
   a. Rounding0
   b. Concept
   c. Undefined
   d. Undefined

139. In mathematics, a _____ in elementary terms is any of a variety of different functions from geometry, such as rotations, reflections and translations.
   a. Thing
   b. Transformation0
   c. Undefined
   d. Undefined

140. A _____ is a function that assigns a number to subsets of a given set.
   a. Thing
   b. Measure0
   c. Undefined
   d. Undefined

141. _____ is the estimation of a physical quantity such as distance, energy, temperature, or time.
   a. Measurement0
   b. Thing
   c. Undefined
   d. Undefined

142. In the mathematical field of numerical analysis, the _____ in some data is the discrepancy between an exact value and some approximation to it.
   a. Thing
   b. Approximation Error0
   c. Undefined
   d. Undefined

143. The _____ of measurement are a globally standardized and modernized form of the metric system.
   a. Units0
   b. Thing
   c. Undefined
   d. Undefined

144. The _____ of a ring R is defined to be the smallest positive integer n such that $n\,a = 0$, for all a in R.
   a. Thing
   b. Characteristic0
   c. Undefined
   d. Undefined

145. _____ is the application of tools and a processing medium to the transformation of raw materials into finished goods for sale.
   a. Manufacturing0
   b. Thing
   c. Undefined
   d. Undefined

146. A _____ is a set of numbers that designate location in a given reference system, such as x,y in a planar _____ system or an x,y,z in a three-dimensional _____ system.
   a. Coordinate0
   b. Thing
   c. Undefined
   d. Undefined

147. In mathematics, a _____ is a two-dimensional manifold or surface that is perfectly flat.
   a. Plane0
   b. Thing
   c. Undefined
   d. Undefined

148. In common philosophical language, a proposition or _____, is the content of an assertion, that is, it is true-or-false and defined by the meaning of a particular piece of language.
   a. Statement0
   b. Concept
   c. Undefined
   d. Undefined

149. _____ is a form of periodic payment from an employer to an employee, which is specified in an employment contract.
   a. Thing
   b. Gross pay0
   c. Undefined
   d. Undefined

150. The payment of _____ as remuneration for services rendered or products sold is a common way to reward sales people.
   a. Thing
   b. Commission0
   c. Undefined
   d. Undefined

Chapter 2. Numbers and Functions

151. A _____ is a form of periodic payment from an employer to an employee, which is specified in an employment contract.
 a. Thing
 b. Salary0
 c. Undefined
 d. Undefined

152. In Euclidean geometry, a _____ is moving every point a constant distance in a specified direction.
 a. Translation0
 b. Concept
 c. Undefined
 d. Undefined

153. An _____ is when two lines intersect somewhere on a plane creating a right angle at intersection
 a. Axes0
 b. Thing
 c. Undefined
 d. Undefined

154. In combinatorial mathematics, a _____ is an un-ordered collection of unique elements.
 a. Concept
 b. Combination0
 c. Undefined
 d. Undefined

155. An _____ is a straight line around which a geometric figure can be rotated.
 a. Axis0
 b. Thing
 c. Undefined
 d. Undefined

156. In mathematical analysis, _____ are objects which generalize functions and probability distributions.
 a. Distribution0
 b. Thing
 c. Undefined
 d. Undefined

157. A _____ is a unit of length in the metric system, equal to one thousand metres, the current SI base unit of length
 a. Thing
 b. Kilometer0
 c. Undefined
 d. Undefined

158. _____ is a function whose values do not vary and thus are constant.
 a. Constant function0
 b. Thing
 c. Undefined
 d. Undefined

159. In mathematics, a _____ is the end result of a division problem. It can also be expressed as the number of times the divisor divides into the dividend.
 a. Quotient0
 b. Thing
 c. Undefined
 d. Undefined

160. Initial objects are also called _____, and terminal objects are also called final.
 a. Thing
 b. Coterminal0
 c. Undefined
 d. Undefined

161. _____ are activities that are governed by a set of rules or customs and often engaged in competitively.
 a. Sports0
 b. Thing
 c. Undefined
 d. Undefined

Chapter 2. Numbers and Functions

162. The _____ is the distance around a closed curve. _____ is a kind of perimeter.
 a. Thing
 b. Circumference0
 c. Undefined
 d. Undefined

163. A _____ is a quantity that denotes the proportional amount or magnitude of one quantity relative to another.
 a. Ratio0
 b. Thing
 c. Undefined
 d. Undefined

164. In mathematics, a _____ is an ordered list of objects. Like a set, it contains members, also called elements or terms, and the number of terms is called the length of the _____. Unlike a set, order matters, and the exact same elements can appear multiple times at different positions in the _____.
 a. Thing
 b. Sequence0
 c. Undefined
 d. Undefined

165. In Euclidean geometry, an _____ is a closed segment of a differentiable curve in the two-dimensional plane; for example, a circular _____ is a segment of a circle.
 a. Concept
 b. Arc0
 c. Undefined
 d. Undefined

Chapter 3. Systems of Linear Equations and Inequalities

1. _____, from Latin meaning "to make progress", is defined in two different ways. Pure economic _____ is the increase in wealth that an investor has from making an investment, taking into consideration all costs associated with that investment including the opportunity cost of capital.
   a. Thing
   b. Profit0
   c. Undefined
   d. Undefined

2. In mathematics, an _____ is a statement about the relative size or order of two objects.
   a. Inequality0
   b. Thing
   c. Undefined
   d. Undefined

3. In mathematics, a _____ is a condition that a solution to an optimization problem must satisfy in order to be acceptable.
   a. Constraint0
   b. Thing
   c. Undefined
   d. Undefined

4. The mathematical concept of a _____ expresses the intuitive idea of deterministic dependence between two quantities, one of which is viewed as primary and the other as secondary. A _____ then is a way to associate a unique output for each input of a specified type, for example, a real number or an element of a given set.
   a. Function0
   b. Thing
   c. Undefined
   d. Undefined

5. The word _____ comes from the Latin word linearis, which means created by lines.
   a. Linear0
   b. Thing
   c. Undefined
   d. Undefined

6. A _____ is an equation in which each term is either a constant or the product of a constant times the first power of a variable.
   a. Thing
   b. Linear equation0
   c. Undefined
   d. Undefined

7. An _____ is a collection of two not necessarily distinct objects, one of which is distinguished as the first coordinate and the other as the second coordinate.
   a. Thing
   b. Ordered pair0
   c. Undefined
   d. Undefined

8. _____ are the basic objects of study in graph theory. Informally speaking, a graph is a set of objects called points, nodes, or vertices connected by links called lines or edges.
   a. Graphs0
   b. Thing
   c. Undefined
   d. Undefined

9. In mathematics, the _____ of two sets A and B is the set that contains all elements of A that also belong to B (or equivalently, all elements of B that also belong to A), but no other elements.
   a. Intersection0
   b. Thing
   c. Undefined
   d. Undefined

Chapter 3. Systems of Linear Equations and Inequalities

10. _____ is often used to describe the measurement of the steepness, incline, gradient, or grade of a straight line. The _____ is defined as the ratio of the "rise" divided by the "run" between two points on a line, or in other words, the ratio of the altitude change to the horizontal distance between any two points on the line.
   a. Thing
   b. Slope0
   c. Undefined
   d. Undefined

11. A _____ is a symbolic representation denoting a quantity or expression. It often represents an "unknown" quantity that has the potential to change.
   a. Thing
   b. Variable0
   c. Undefined
   d. Undefined

12. _____ are a set of equations containing multiple variables.
   a. Thing
   b. Systems of equations0
   c. Undefined
   d. Undefined

13. In geometry, _____ lines are two lines that share one or more common points.
   a. Intersecting0
   b. Thing
   c. Undefined
   d. Undefined

14. In mathematics, a _____ is a constant multiplicative factor of a certain object. The object can be such things as a variable, a vector, a function, etc. For example, the _____ of $9x^2$ is 9.
   a. Thing
   b. Coefficient0
   c. Undefined
   d. Undefined

15. _____ forms part of thinking. Considered the most complex of all intellectual functions, _____ has been defined as higher-order cognitive process that requires the modulation and control of more routine or fundamental skills.
   a. Thing
   b. Problem solving0
   c. Undefined
   d. Undefined

16. _____ is a kind of property which exists as magnitude or multitude. It is among the basic classes of things along with quality, substance, change, and relation.
   a. Amount0
   b. Thing
   c. Undefined
   d. Undefined

17. In mathematics, a _____ is an n-tuple with n being 3.
   a. Triple0
   b. Thing
   c. Undefined
   d. Undefined

18. In chemistry, a _____ is substance made by combining two or more different materials in such a way that no chemical reaction occurs.
   a. Mixture0
   b. Thing
   c. Undefined
   d. Undefined

19. An _____ is a combination of numbers, operators, grouping symbols and/or free variables and bound variables arranged in a meaningful way which can be evaluated..

Chapter 3. Systems of Linear Equations and Inequalities

    a. Thing
    b. Expression0
    c. Undefined
    d. Undefined

20. _____ is the distance around a given two-dimensional object. As a general rule, the _____ of a polygon can always be calculated by adding all the length of the sides together. So, the formula for triangles is P = a + b + c, where a, b and c stand for each side of it. For quadrilaterals the equation is P = a + b + c + d. For equilateral polygons, P = na, where n is the number of sides and a is the side length.
    a. Thing
    b. Perimeter0
    c. Undefined
    d. Undefined

21. In the scientific method, an _____ (Latin: ex-+-periri, "of (or from) trying"), is a set of actions and observations, performed in the context of solving a particular problem or question, in order to support or falsify a hypothesis or research concerning phenomena.
    a. Experiment0
    b. Thing
    c. Undefined
    d. Undefined

22. _____ are activities that are governed by a set of rules or customs and often engaged in competitively.
    a. Sports0
    b. Thing
    c. Undefined
    d. Undefined

23. In _____ algebra, a *-ring is an associative ring with an antilinear, antiautomorphism * : A ¨ A which is an involution.
    a. Star0
    b. Thing
    c. Undefined
    d. Undefined

24. A _____ is a one-dimensional picture in which the integers are shown as specially-marked points evenly spaced on a line.
    a. Number line0
    b. Thing
    c. Undefined
    d. Undefined

25. In common philosophical language, a proposition or _____, is the content of an assertion, that is, it is true-or-false and defined by the meaning of a particular piece of language.
    a. Concept
    b. Statement0
    c. Undefined
    d. Undefined

26. _____ element of an element x with respect to a binary operation * with identity element e is an element y such that x * y = y * x = e. In particular,
    a. Thing
    b. Inverse0
    c. Undefined
    d. Undefined

27. _____ systems represent systems whose behavior is not expressible as a sum of the behaviors of its descriptors.
    a. Thing
    b. Nonlinear0
    c. Undefined
    d. Undefined

28. A _____ represents a system whose behavior is not expressible as a sum of the behaviors of its descriptors.

Chapter 3. Systems of Linear Equations and Inequalities

    a. Thing
    c. Undefined
    b. Nonlinear system0
    d. Undefined

29. The Gaussian _____ is an algorithm which can be used to determine the solutions of a system of linear equations, to find the rank of a matrix, and to calculate the inverse of an invertible square matrix.
    a. Thing
    c. Undefined
    b. Elimination method0
    d. Undefined

30. _____ is a notation for writing numbers that is often used by scientists and mathematicians to make it easier to write large and small numbers.
    a. Thing
    c. Undefined
    b. Scientific notation0
    d. Undefined

31. In mathematics, the additive inverse, or _____ of a number n is the number that, when added to n, yields zero. The additive inverse of n is denoted −n. For example, 7 is −7, because 7 + (−7) = 0, and the additive inverse of −0.3 is 0.3, because −0.3 + 0.3 = 0.
    a. Thing
    c. Undefined
    b. Opposite0
    d. Undefined

32. In mathematics and the mathematical sciences, a _____ is a fixed, but possibly unspecified, value. This is in contrast to a variable, which is not fixed.
    a. Constant0
    c. Undefined
    b. Thing
    d. Undefined

33. In mathematics, the _____ of a number n is the number that, when added to n, yields zero. The _____ of n is denoted −n. For example, 7 is −7, because 7 + (−7) = 0, and the _____ of −0.3 is 0.3, because −0.3 + 0.3 = 0.
    a. Additive inverse0
    c. Undefined
    b. Thing
    d. Undefined

34. The _____ is used to discard one of the variables in an equation, only to replace it with the actual value when solving multiple equations.
    a. Substitution method0
    c. Undefined
    b. Thing
    d. Undefined

35. A _____ is a set of numbers that designate location in a given reference system, such as x,y in a planar _____ system or an x,y,z in a three-dimensional _____ system.
    a. Thing
    c. Undefined
    b. Coordinate0
    d. Undefined

36. In mathematics, the conjugate _____ or adjoint matrix of an m-by-n matrix A with complex entries is the n-by-m matrix A* obtained from A by taking the transpose and then taking the complex conjugate of each entry.
    a. Pairs0
    c. Undefined
    b. Thing
    d. Undefined

Chapter 3. Systems of Linear Equations and Inequalities

37. _____ is the study of geometry using the principles of algebra. _____ can be explained more simply: it is concerned with defining geometrical shapes in a numerical way and extracting numerical information from that representation.
   a. Analytic geometry0
   b. Thing
   c. Undefined
   d. Undefined

38. _____ or investing is a term with several closely-related meanings in business management, finance and economics, related to saving or deferring consumption.
   a. Thing
   b. Investment0
   c. Undefined
   d. Undefined

39. The _____ of measurement are a globally standardized and modernized form of the metric system.
   a. Thing
   b. Units0
   c. Undefined
   d. Undefined

40. _____ interest refers to the fact that whenever interest is calculated, it is based not only on the original principal, but also on any unpaid interest that has been added to the principal.
   a. Compound0
   b. Thing
   c. Undefined
   d. Undefined

41. In arithmetic and algebra, when a number or expression is both preceded and followed by a binary operation, an _____ is required for which operation should be applied first.
   a. Order of operations0
   b. Thing
   c. Undefined
   d. Undefined

42. In mathematics, a _____ function in the sense of algebraic geometry is an everywhere-defined, polynomial function on an algebraic variety V with values in the field K over which V is defined.
   a. Thing
   b. Regular0
   c. Undefined
   d. Undefined

43. _____ is the application of tools and a processing medium to the transformation of raw materials into finished goods for sale.
   a. Thing
   b. Manufacturing0
   c. Undefined
   d. Undefined

44. _____ are a measure of time.
   a. Minutes0
   b. Thing
   c. Undefined
   d. Undefined

45. U.S. liquid _____ is legally defined as 231 cubic inches, and is equal to 3.785411784 litres or abotu 0.13368 cubic feet. This is the most common definition of a _____. The U.S. fluid ounce is defined as 1/128 of a U.S. _____.
   a. Thing
   b. Gallon0
   c. Undefined
   d. Undefined

46. In mathematical analysis and related areas of mathematics, a set is called _____, if it is, in a certain sense, of finite size.
   a. Bounded0
   b. Thing
   c. Undefined
   d. Undefined

47. In mathematics, a _____ is a two-dimensional manifold or surface that is perfectly flat.
   a. Thing
   b. Plane0
   c. Undefined
   d. Undefined

48. Acid _____ ratio measures the ability of a company to use its near cash or quick assets to immediately extinguish its current liabilities.
   a. Thing
   b. Test0
   c. Undefined
   d. Undefined

49. In mathematics, _____ geometry was the traditional name for the geometry of three-dimensional Euclidean space — for practical purposes the kind of space we live in.
   a. Thing
   b. Solid0
   c. Undefined
   d. Undefined

50. _____ is the transport of people on a trip/journey or the process or time involved in a person or object moving from one location to another.
   a. Thing
   b. Travel0
   c. Undefined
   d. Undefined

51. In mathematics, an inequality is a statement about the relative size or order of two objects. For example 14 > 10, or 14 is _____ 10.
   a. Thing
   b. Greater than0
   c. Undefined
   d. Undefined

52. The word _____ comes from the 15th Century Latin word discretus which means separate.
   a. Discrete0
   b. Thing
   c. Undefined
   d. Undefined

53. In mathematics, a _____ can mean either an element of the set {1, 2, 3, ...} (i.e the positive integers) or an element of the set {0, 1, 2, 3, ...} (i.e. the non-negative integers).
   a. Concept
   b. Whole number0
   c. Undefined
   d. Undefined

54. In mathematics, the _____ of a function is the set of all "output" values produced by that function. Given a function $f: A \to B$, the _____ of f, is defined to be the set $\{x \in B : x = f(a) \text{ for some } a \in A\}$.
   a. Thing
   b. Range0
   c. Undefined
   d. Undefined

55. A _____ consists of one quarter of the coordinate plane.

Chapter 3. Systems of Linear Equations and Inequalities

a. Thing
b. Quadrant0
c. Undefined
d. Undefined

56. An _____ is when two lines intersect somewhere on a plane creating a right angle at intersection
   a. Axes0
   b. Thing
   c. Undefined
   d. Undefined

57. In mathematics, an _____, mean, or central tendency of a data set refers to a measure of the "middle" or "expected" value of the data set.
   a. Concept
   b. Average0
   c. Undefined
   d. Undefined

58. _____ is a physical property of a system that underlies the common notions of hot and cold; something that is hotter has the greater _____.
   a. Thing
   b. Temperature0
   c. Undefined
   d. Undefined

59. In mathematics, there are several meanings of _____ depending on the subject.
   a. Degree0
   b. Thing
   c. Undefined
   d. Undefined

60. In geometry, a _____ is a special kind of point, usually a corner of a polygon, polyhedron, or higher dimensional polytope. In the geometry of curves a _____ is a point of where the first derivative of curvature is zero. In graph theory, a _____ is the fundamental unit out of which graphs are formed
   a. Vertex0
   b. Thing
   c. Undefined
   d. Undefined

61. A _____ is a polygon with four sides and four vertices.
   a. Quadrilateral0
   b. Thing
   c. Undefined
   d. Undefined

62. A _____ is a four-sided plane figure that has two sets of opposite parallel sides.
   a. Concept
   b. Parallelogram0
   c. Undefined
   d. Undefined

63. In combinatorial mathematics, a _____ is an un-ordered collection of unique elements.
   a. Concept
   b. Combination0
   c. Undefined
   d. Undefined

64. The _____ are the only integral domain whose positive elements are well-ordered, and in which order is preserved by addition. Like the natural numbers, the _____ form a countably infinite set. The set of all _____ is usually denoted in mathematics by a boldface Z .
   a. Integers0
   b. Thing
   c. Undefined
   d. Undefined

Chapter 3. Systems of Linear Equations and Inequalities

65. In mathematics, _____ problems involve the optimization of a linear objective function, subject to linear equality and inequality constraints.
    a. Thing
    b. Linear programming0
    c. Undefined
    d. Undefined

66. _____ is a business term for the amount of money that a company receives from its activities in a given period, mostly from sales of products and/or services to customers
    a. Thing
    b. Revenue0
    c. Undefined
    d. Undefined

67. In optimization, a candidate solution is a member of a set of possible solutions to a given problem. A candidate solution does not have to be a likely or reasonable solution to the problem. The space of all candidate solutions is called the _____, feasible set, search space, or solution space.
    a. Feasible region0
    b. Thing
    c. Undefined
    d. Undefined

68. _____ is a mathematical science pertaining to the collection, analysis, interpretation or explanation, and presentation of data. It is applicable to a wide variety of academic disciplines, from the physical and social sciences to the humanities.
    a. Statistics0
    b. Thing
    c. Undefined
    d. Undefined

69. A _____ signifies a point or points of probability on a subject e.g., the _____ of creativity, which allows for the formation of rule or norm or law by interpretation of the phenomena events that can be created.
    a. Thing
    b. Principle0
    c. Undefined
    d. Undefined

70. The _____, the average in everyday English, which is also called the arithmetic _____ (and is distinguished from the geometric _____ or harmonic _____). The average is also called the sample _____. The expected value of a random variable, which is also called the population _____.
    a. Mean0
    b. Thing
    c. Undefined
    d. Undefined

71. A _____ function curves downwards. The graph of a _____ function of one variable remains above its tangents and below its cords.
    a. Thing
    b. Convex0
    c. Undefined
    d. Undefined

72. In geometry, a _____ is a simple polygon whose interior is a convex set.
    a. Convex polygon0
    b. Thing
    c. Undefined
    d. Undefined

73. In geometry a _____ is a plane figure that is bounded by a closed path or circuit, composed of a finite number of sequential line segments.

Chapter 3. Systems of Linear Equations and Inequalities

    a. Polygon0
    b. Thing
    c. Undefined
    d. Undefined

74. In geometry, a line _____ is a part of a line that is bounded by two end points, and contains every point on the line between its end points.
    a. Concept
    b. Segment0
    c. Undefined
    d. Undefined

75. A _____ is a part of a line that is bounded by two end points, and contains every point on the line between its end points.
    a. Line segment0
    b. Thing
    c. Undefined
    d. Undefined

76. In geometry, _____ are plane figures that are bounded by a closed path or circuit, composed of a finite number of sequential line segments.
    a. Polygons0
    b. Thing
    c. Undefined
    d. Undefined

77. In mathematics, _____ are two-dimensional manifolds or surfaces that are perfectly flat.
    a. Planes0
    b. Thing
    c. Undefined
    d. Undefined

78. _____ is the level of functional and/or metabolic efficiency of an organism at both the micro level.
    a. Health0
    b. Thing
    c. Undefined
    d. Undefined

79. An _____ is a term used to describe an allocation of money from one person to another.
    a. Thing
    b. Allowance0
    c. Undefined
    d. Undefined

80. _____ is the production of food, feed, fiber, fuel and other goods by the systematic raizing of plants and animals.
    a. Thing
    b. Agriculture0
    c. Undefined
    d. Undefined

81. In mathematics, a _____ of a k-place relation $L \subseteq X_1 \times \ldots \times X_k$ is one of the sets X_j, $1 \le j \le k$. In the special case where k = 2 and $L \subseteq X_1 \times X_2$ is a function $L : X_1 \to X_2$, it is conventional to refer to X_1 as the _____ of the function and to refer to X_2 as the codomain of the function.
    a. Domain0
    b. Thing
    c. Undefined
    d. Undefined

82. In mathematics, factorization (British English: factorisation) or factoring is the decomposition of an object (for example, a number, a polynomial, or a matrix) into a product of other objects, or _____, which when multiplied together give the original.
    a. Factors0
    b. Thing
    c. Undefined
    d. Undefined

Chapter 3. Systems of Linear Equations and Inequalities

83. _____ statistics are statistics that estimate population parameters.
    a. Thing
    b. Parametric0
    c. Undefined
    d. Undefined

84. In mathematics, _____ bear slight similarity to functions: they allow one to use arbitrary values, called parameters, in place of independent variables in equations, which in turn provide values for dependent variables. A simple kinematical example is when one uses a time parameter to determine the position, velocity, and other information about a body in motion.
    a. Thing
    b. Parametric equations0
    c. Undefined
    d. Undefined

85. A _____ is a special kind of ratio, indicating a relationship between two measurements with different units, such as miles to gallons or cents to pounds.
    a. Rate0
    b. Thing
    c. Undefined
    d. Undefined

86. In astronomy, geography, geometry and related sciences and contexts, a plane is said to be _____ at a given point if it is locally perpendicular to the gradient of the gravity field, i.e., with the direction of the gravitational force at that point.
    a. Horizontal0
    b. Thing
    c. Undefined
    d. Undefined

87. In geometry, an _____ of a triangle is a straight line through a vertex and perpendicular to (i.e. forming a right angle with) the opposite side or an extension of the opposite side.
    a. Concept
    b. Altitude0
    c. Undefined
    d. Undefined

88. In statistics, _____ means the most frequent value assumed by a random variable, or occurring in a sampling of a random variable.
    a. Concept
    b. Mode0
    c. Undefined
    d. Undefined

89. A _____ function is a function for which, intuitively, small changes in the input result in small changes in the output.
    a. Event
    b. Continuous0
    c. Undefined
    d. Undefined

90. A _____ is the quantity that defines certain relatively constant characteristics of systems or functions..
    a. Parameter0
    b. Thing
    c. Undefined
    d. Undefined

91. In linear algebra, the _____ of an n-by-n square matrix A is defined to be the sum of the elements on the main diagonal of A,
    a. Trace0
    b. Thing
    c. Undefined
    d. Undefined

Chapter 3. Systems of Linear Equations and Inequalities

92. In geographic information systems, a _____ comprises an entity with a geographic location, typically determined by points, arcs, or polygons. Carriageways and cadastres exemplify _____ data.
   a. Feature0
   b. Thing
   c. Undefined
   d. Undefined

93. In elementary algebra, an _____ is a set that contains every real number between two indicated numbers and may contain the two numbers themselves.
   a. Interval0
   b. Thing
   c. Undefined
   d. Undefined

94. In mathematics, a _____ in elementary terms is any of a variety of different functions from geometry, such as rotations, reflections and translations.
   a. Thing
   b. Transformation0
   c. Undefined
   d. Undefined

95. _____ of an object is its speed in a particular direction.
   a. Thing
   b. Velocity0
   c. Undefined
   d. Undefined

96. Initial objects are also called _____, and terminal objects are also called final.
   a. Thing
   b. Coterminal0
   c. Undefined
   d. Undefined

97. In botany, _____ are above-ground plant organs specialized for photosynthesis. Their characteristics are typically analyzed by using Fiobonacci's sequences.
   a. Thing
   b. Leaves0
   c. Undefined
   d. Undefined

98. The metre (or _____, see spelling differences) is a measure of length. It is the basic unit of length in the metric system and in the International System of Units (SI), used around the world for general and scientific purposes.
   a. Meter0
   b. Concept
   c. Undefined
   d. Undefined

99. In topology and related areas of mathematics a _____ or Moore-Smith sequence is a generalization of a sequence, intended to unify the various notions of limit and generalize them to arbitrary topological spaces.
   a. Net0
   b. Thing
   c. Undefined
   d. Undefined

100. _____ is the path a moving object follows through space.
   a. Projectile motion0
   b. Thing
   c. Undefined
   d. Undefined

101. The _____ is a unit of plane angle. It is represented by the symbol "rad" or, more rarely, by the superscript c (for "circular measure"). For example, an angle of 1.2 radians would be written "1.2 rad" or "1.2c" (second symbol can produce confusion with centigrads).

a. Radian0
b. Thing
c. Undefined
d. Undefined

102. In mathematics, a _____ or rhodonea curve is a sinusoid plotted in polar coordinates.
   a. Rose0
   b. Thing
   c. Undefined
   d. Undefined

103. In plane geometry, a _____ is a polygon with four equal sides, four right angles, and parallel opposite sides. In algebra, the _____ of a number is that number multiplied by itself.
   a. Square0
   b. Thing
   c. Undefined
   d. Undefined

104. Compass and straightedge or ruler-and-compass _____ is the _____ of lengths or angles using only an idealized ruler and compass.
   a. Thing
   b. Construction0
   c. Undefined
   d. Undefined

105. Statistical _____ is a statistical procedure in which individual items are placed into groups based on quantitative information on one or more characteristics inherent in the items and based on a training set of previously labeled items.
   a. Classification0
   b. Thing
   c. Undefined
   d. Undefined

106. Multiple Signal Classification, also known as _____, is an algorithm used for frequency estimation and emitter location.
   a. Thing
   b. Music0
   c. Undefined
   d. Undefined

107. A _____ is a plan of action to guide decisions and actions.
   a. Policy0
   b. Thing
   c. Undefined
   d. Undefined

108. In geometry, the _____ of an object is a point in some sense in the middle of the object.
   a. Center0
   b. Thing
   c. Undefined
   d. Undefined

109. In economics, _____ describe market relations between prospective sellers and buyers of a good.
   a. Supply and demand0
   b. Thing
   c. Undefined
   d. Undefined

110. In economics, economic _____ is simply a state of the world where economic forces are balanced and in the absence of external influences the values of economic variables will not change.
   a. Equilibrium0
   b. Thing
   c. Undefined
   d. Undefined

111. _____ is the price at which the quantity demanded of a good or service is equal to the quantity supplied.

Chapter 3. Systems of Linear Equations and Inequalities

a. Thing
b. Equilibrium price0
c. Undefined
d. Undefined

112. The _____ a graphing calculator allow the user to change the view of the graph.
a. Thing
b. Zoom features on0
c. Undefined
d. Undefined

113. In mathematical optimization theory, the _____, created by the North American mathematician George Dantzig in 1947, is a popular technique for numerical solution of the linear programming problem.
a. Simplex algorithm0
b. Thing
c. Undefined
d. Undefined

114. _____ is a branch of mathematics concerning the study of structure, relation and quantity.
a. Algebra0
b. Concept
c. Undefined
d. Undefined

115. In geometry, a _____ (Greek words diairo = divide and metro = measure) of a circle is any straight line segment that passes through the centre and whose endpoints are on the circular boundary, or, in more modern usage, the length of such a line segment. When using the word in the more modern sense, one speaks of the _____ rather than a _____, because all diameters of a circle have the same length. This length is twice the radius. The _____ of a circle is also the longest chord that the circle has.
a. Thing
b. Diameter0
c. Undefined
d. Undefined

116. In mathematics, a _____ is an ordered list of objects. Like a set, it contains members, also called elements or terms, and the number of terms is called the length of the _____. Unlike a set, order matters, and the exact same elements can appear multiple times at different positions in the _____.
a. Sequence0
b. Thing
c. Undefined
d. Undefined

Chapter 4. Matrices

1. In Graph theory, a _____ is a digraph with weighted edges.
   a. Network0
   b. Concept
   c. Undefined
   d. Undefined

2. In computer science an _____ is a data structure that consists of a group of elements having a single name that are accessed by indexing. In most programming languages each element has the same data type and the _____ occupies a continuous area of storage.
   a. Array0
   b. Thing
   c. Undefined
   d. Undefined

3. In mathematics, a _____ is a rectangular table of numbers or, more generally, a table consisting of abstract quantities that can be added and multiplied.
   a. Matrix0
   b. Thing
   c. Undefined
   d. Undefined

4. _____ is a list of goods and materials, or those goods and materials themselves, held available in stock by a business
   a. Thing
   b. Inventory0
   c. Undefined
   d. Undefined

5. _____ is a synonym for information.
   a. Data0
   b. Thing
   c. Undefined
   d. Undefined

6. In mathematics, a _____ is the result of multiplying, or an expression that identifies factors to be multiplied.
   a. Product0
   b. Thing
   c. Undefined
   d. Undefined

7. A _____ is the result of the addition of a set of numbers. The numbers may be natural numbers, complex numbers, matrices, or still more complicated objects. An infinite _____ is a subtle procedure known as a series.
   a. Sum0
   b. Thing
   c. Undefined
   d. Undefined

8. In linear algebra, real numbers are called scalars and relate to vectors in a vector space through the operation of _____ multiplication, in which a vector can be multiplied by a number to produce another vector.
   a. Thing
   b. Scalar0
   c. Undefined
   d. Undefined

9. A _____ is a deliberate process for transforming one or more inputs into one or more results.
   a. Calculation0
   b. Thing
   c. Undefined
   d. Undefined

10. In mathematics, _____ is an elementary arithmetic operation. When one of the numbers is a whole number, _____ is the repeated sum of the other number.
    a. Thing
    b. Multiplication0
    c. Undefined
    d. Undefined

Chapter 4. Matrices

11. In mathematics, a _____ may be described informally as a number that can be given by an infinite decimal representation.
    a. Thing
    b. Real number0
    c. Undefined
    d. Undefined

12. _____ is one of the basic operations defining a vector space in linear algebra.
    a. Thing
    b. Scalar multiplication0
    c. Undefined
    d. Undefined

13. An _____ is an equality that remains true regardless of the values of any variables that appear within it, to distinguish it from an equality which is true under more particular conditions.
    a. Thing
    b. Identity0
    c. Undefined
    d. Undefined

14. In mathematics, the _____ inverse, or opposite, of a number n is the number that, when added to n, yields zero. The _____ inverse of n is denoted −n.
    a. Thing
    b. Additive0
    c. Undefined
    d. Undefined

15. In mathematics the _____ of a set which is equipped with the operation of addition is an element which, when added to any other element x in the set, yields x.
    a. Concept
    b. Additive identity0
    c. Undefined
    d. Undefined

16. A _____ is a set of numbers that designate location in a given reference system, such as x,y in a planar _____ system or an x,y,z in a three-dimensional _____ system.
    a. Thing
    b. Coordinate0
    c. Undefined
    d. Undefined

17. In mathematics, the additive inverse, or _____ of a number n is the number that, when added to n, yields zero. The additive inverse of n is denoted −n. For example, 7 is −7, because 7 + (−7) = 0, and the additive inverse of −0.3 is 0.3, because −0.3 + 0.3 = 0.
    a. Thing
    b. Opposite0
    c. Undefined
    d. Undefined

18. In mathematics, a _____ is a two-dimensional manifold or surface that is perfectly flat.
    a. Thing
    b. Plane0
    c. Undefined
    d. Undefined

19. In geometry a _____ is a plane figure that is bounded by a closed path or circuit, composed of a finite number of sequential line segments.
    a. Polygon0
    b. Thing
    c. Undefined
    d. Undefined

20. _____ element of an element x with respect to a binary operation * with identity element e is an element y such that x * y = y * x = e. In particular,

a. Thing
b. Inverse0
c. Undefined
d. Undefined

21. In mathematics, the _____ of a number n is the number that, when added to n, yields zero. The _____ of n is denoted −n. For example, 7 is −7, because 7 + (−7) = 0, and the _____ of −0.3 is 0.3, because −0.3 + 0.3 = 0.
   a. Thing
   b. Additive inverse0
   c. Undefined
   d. Undefined

22. In mathematics, _____ is a part of the set theoretic notion of function.
   a. Thing
   b. Image0
   c. Undefined
   d. Undefined

23. A _____ is a polygon with four sides and four vertices.
   a. Quadrilateral0
   b. Thing
   c. Undefined
   d. Undefined

24. In Euclidean geometry, a uniform _____ is a linear transformation that enlargers or diminishes objects, and whose _____ factor is the same in all directions. This is also called homothethy.
   a. Thing
   b. Scale0
   c. Undefined
   d. Undefined

25. In mathematics, a _____ in elementary terms is any of a variety of different functions from geometry, such as rotations, reflections and translations.
   a. Transformation0
   b. Thing
   c. Undefined
   d. Undefined

26. In plane geometry, a _____ is a polygon with four equal sides, four right angles, and parallel opposite sides. In algebra, the _____ of a number is that number multiplied by itself.
   a. Thing
   b. Square0
   c. Undefined
   d. Undefined

27. A _____, is a symbolized depiction of space which highlights relations between components of that space. Most usually a _____ is a two-dimensional, geometrically accurate representation of a three-dimensional space.
   a. Thing
   b. Map0
   c. Undefined
   d. Undefined

28. In mathematics, a matrix can be thought of as each row or _____ being a vector. Hence, a space formed by row vectors or _____ vectors are said to be a row space or a _____ space.
   a. Column0
   b. Concept
   c. Undefined
   d. Undefined

29. In probability theory, _____ are various sets of outcomes (a subset of the sample space) to which a probability is assigned.
   a. Thing
   b. Events0
   c. Undefined
   d. Undefined

Chapter 4. Matrices

30. Multiple Signal Classification, also known as _____, is an algorithm used for frequency estimation and emitter location.
    a. Thing
    b. Music0
    c. Undefined
    d. Undefined

31. In mathematics, a subset of Euclidean space R^n is called _____ if it is closed and bounded.
    a. Compact0
    b. Thing
    c. Undefined
    d. Undefined

32. _____ is often used to describe the measurement of the steepness, incline, gradient, or grade of a straight line. The _____ is defined as the ratio of the "rise" divided by the "run" between two points on a line, or in other words, the ratio of the altitude change to the horizontal distance between any two points on the line.
    a. Slope0
    b. Thing
    c. Undefined
    d. Undefined

33. _____ statistics are statistics that estimate population parameters.
    a. Parametric0
    b. Thing
    c. Undefined
    d. Undefined

34. In mathematics, _____ bear slight similarity to functions: they allow one to use arbitrary values, called parameters, in place of independent variables in equations, which in turn provide values for dependent variables. A simple kinematical example is when one uses a time parameter to determine the position, velocity, and other information about a body in motion.
    a. Thing
    b. Parametric equations0
    c. Undefined
    d. Undefined

35. Equivalence is the condition of being _____ or essentially equal.
    a. Equivalent0
    b. Thing
    c. Undefined
    d. Undefined

36. In mathematics, particularly linear algebra, two matrices A and B are said to be _____ if it is possible to transform A into B by a sequence of elementary operations.
    a. Thing
    b. Equivalent matrices0
    c. Undefined
    d. Undefined

37. The word _____ comes from the Latin word linearis, which means created by lines.
    a. Thing
    b. Linear0
    c. Undefined
    d. Undefined

38. A _____ is an equation in which each term is either a constant or the product of a constant times the first power of a variable.
    a. Thing
    b. Linear equation0
    c. Undefined
    d. Undefined

39. In mathematics, a _____ is a mathematical statement which appears likely to be true, but has not been formally proven to be true under the rules of mathematical logic.

a. Concept
b. Conjecture0
c. Undefined
d. Undefined

40. In mathematics, a set is called _____ if there is a bijection between the set and some set of the form {1, 2, ..., n} where n is a natural number.
   a. Thing
   b. Finite0
   c. Undefined
   d. Undefined

41. In mathematics, a _____ occurs if there is a bijection between the set and some set of the form 1, 2, ..., n where n is a natural number.
   a. Concept
   b. Finite set0
   c. Undefined
   d. Undefined

42. _____ is the transport of people on a trip/journey or the process or time involved in a person or object moving from one location to another.
   a. Thing
   b. Travel0
   c. Undefined
   d. Undefined

43. In geometry, a _____ is a special kind of point, usually a corner of a polygon, polyhedron, or higher dimensional polytope. In the geometry of curves a _____ is a point of where the first derivative of curvature is zero. In graph theory, a _____ is the fundamental unit out of which graphs are formed
   a. Thing
   b. Vertex0
   c. Undefined
   d. Undefined

44. The _____, the average in everyday English, which is also called the arithmetic _____ (and is distinguished from the geometric _____ or harmonic _____). The average is also called the sample _____. The expected value of a random variable, which is also called the population _____.
   a. Mean0
   b. Thing
   c. Undefined
   d. Undefined

45. _____ of a finite directed or undirected graph G on n vertices is the n × n matrix where the nondiagonal entry aij is the number of edges from vertex i to vertex j, and the diagonal entry aii is either twice the number of loops at vertex i or just the number of loops usages differ, depending on the mathematical needs; this article follows the former convention for undirected graphs, though directed graphs always follow the latter.
   a. Adjacency matrix0
   b. Thing
   c. Undefined
   d. Undefined

46. _____ is the study of geometry using the principles of algebra. _____ can be explained more simply: it is concerned with defining geometrical shapes in a numerical way and extracting numerical information from that representation.
   a. Analytic geometry0
   b. Thing
   c. Undefined
   d. Undefined

47. In chemistry, a _____ is substance made by combining two or more different materials in such a way that no chemical reaction occurs.

a. Thing
b. Mixture0
c. Undefined
d. Undefined

48. In mathematics, a _____ function in the sense of algebraic geometry is an everywhere-defined, polynomial function on an algebraic variety V with values in the field K over which V is defined.
   a. Thing
   b. Regular0
   c. Undefined
   d. Undefined

49. In mathematics, a _____ can mean either an element of the set {1, 2, 3, ...} (i.e the positive integers) or an element of the set {0, 1, 2, 3, ...} (i.e. the non-negative integers).
   a. Concept
   b. Whole number0
   c. Undefined
   d. Undefined

50. _____ has many meanings, most of which simply .
   a. Thing
   b. Power0
   c. Undefined
   d. Undefined

51. In mathematical logic, a Gödel numbering (or Gödel _____) is a function that assigns to each symbol and well-formed formula of some formal language a unique natural number called its Gödel number.
   a. Code0
   b. Thing
   c. Undefined
   d. Undefined

52. In physics, _____ is an influence that may cause an object to accelerate. It may be experienced as a lift, a push, or a pull. The actual acceleration of the body is determined by the vector sum of all forces acting on it, known as net _____ or resultant _____.
   a. Thing
   b. Force0
   c. Undefined
   d. Undefined

53. In linear algebra, the _____ of a square matrix is the diagonal which runs from the top left corner to the bottom right corner.
   a. Thing
   b. Main diagonal0
   c. Undefined
   d. Undefined

54. A _____ can refer to a line joining two nonadjacent vertices of a polygon or polyhedron, or in some contexts any upward or downward sloping line. .
   a. Diagonal0
   b. Thing
   c. Undefined
   d. Undefined

55. In algebra, a _____ is a function depending on *n* that associates a scalar, det(A), to every *n×n* square matrix A.
   a. Thing
   b. Determinant0
   c. Undefined
   d. Undefined

56. In mathematics, the idea of _____ generalises the concepts of negation, in relation to addition, and reciprocal, in relation to multiplication.

a. Inverse element0
b. Thing
c. Undefined
d. Undefined

57. In mathematics, an _____ is a statement about the relative size or order of two objects.
   a. Inequality0
   b. Thing
   c. Undefined
   d. Undefined

58. In geometry, the _____ of an object is a point in some sense in the middle of the object.
   a. Thing
   b. Center0
   c. Undefined
   d. Undefined

59. In mathematics, _____ is the decomposition of an object into a product of other objects, or factors, which when multiplied together give the original.
   a. Factoring0
   b. Thing
   c. Undefined
   d. Undefined

60. In mathematics, factorization (British English: factorisation) or factoring is the decomposition of an object (for example, a number, a polynomial, or a matrix) into a product of other objects, or _____, which when multiplied together give the original.
   a. Factors0
   b. Thing
   c. Undefined
   d. Undefined

61. In mathematics, a _____ number (or a _____) is a natural number that has exactly two (distinct) natural number divisors, which are 1 and the _____ number itself.
   a. Prime0
   b. Thing
   c. Undefined
   d. Undefined

62. _____ was proposed in response to traditional curriculum-driven education. In _____ environments, students interact in purposely structured heterogeneous group to support the learning of one self and others in the same group.
   a. Concept
   b. Cooperative learning0
   c. Undefined
   d. Undefined

63. In mathematics, computing, linguistics, and related disciplines, an _____ is a finite list of well-defined instructions for accomplishing some task which, given an initial state, will terminate in a defined end-state.
   a. Concept
   b. Algorithm0
   c. Undefined
   d. Undefined

64. In mathematics, a _____ is the end result of a division problem. It can also be expressed as the number of times the divisor divides into the dividend.
   a. Quotient0
   b. Thing
   c. Undefined
   d. Undefined

65. A _____ is the part of the dividend that is left over when the dividend is not evenly divisible by the divisor.

Chapter 4. Matrices

    a. Remainder0
    b. Thing
    c. Undefined
    d. Undefined

66. _____ or investing is a term with several closely-related meanings in business management, finance and economics, related to saving or deferring consumption.
    a. Investment0
    b. Thing
    c. Undefined
    d. Undefined

67. _____ is the fee paid on borrowed money.
    a. Thing
    b. Interest0
    c. Undefined
    d. Undefined

68. In mathematics, a _____ is a constant multiplicative factor of a certain object. The object can be such things as a variable, a vector, a function, etc. For example, the _____ of $9x^2$ is 9.
    a. Coefficient0
    b. Thing
    c. Undefined
    d. Undefined

69. In linear algebra, the _____ refers to a matrix consisting of the coefficients of the variables in a set of linear equations.
    a. Thing
    b. Coefficient matrix0
    c. Undefined
    d. Undefined

70. In mathematics and the mathematical sciences, a _____ is a fixed, but possibly unspecified, value. This is in contrast to a variable, which is not fixed.
    a. Constant0
    b. Thing
    c. Undefined
    d. Undefined

71. A _____ is a symbolic representation denoting a quantity or expression. It often represents an "unknown" quantity that has the potential to change.
    a. Thing
    b. Variable0
    c. Undefined
    d. Undefined

72. A _____ is a special kind of ratio, indicating a relationship between two measurements with different units, such as miles to gallons or cents to pounds.
    a. Rate0
    b. Thing
    c. Undefined
    d. Undefined

73. _____ is a kind of property which exists as magnitude or multitude. It is among the basic classes of things along with quality, substance, change, and relation.
    a. Amount0
    b. Thing
    c. Undefined
    d. Undefined

74. A _____ is one of the basic shapes of geometry: a polygon with three vertices and three sides which are straight line segments.

Chapter 4. Matrices

a. Triangle0
b. Thing
c. Undefined
d. Undefined

75. A _____ is a function that assigns a number to subsets of a given set.
    a. Measure0
    b. Thing
    c. Undefined
    d. Undefined

76. In mathematics, an _____, mean, or central tendency of a data set refers to a measure of the "middle" or "expected" value of the data set.
    a. Concept
    b. Average0
    c. Undefined
    d. Undefined

77. In mathematics, the _____ of a function is the set of all "output" values produced by that function. Given a function $f : A \rightarrow B$, the _____ of f, is defined to be the set $\{x \in B : x = f(a) \text{ for some } a \in A\}$.
    a. Range0
    b. Thing
    c. Undefined
    d. Undefined

78. In mathematics, a _____ of a k-place relation $L \subseteq X_1 \times \ldots \times X_k$ is one of the sets X_j, $1 \leq j \leq k$. In the special case where k = 2 and $L \subseteq X_1 \times X_2$ is a function $L : X_1 \rightarrow X_2$, it is conventional to refer to X_1 as the _____ of the function and to refer to X_2 as the codomain of the function.
    a. Domain0
    b. Thing
    c. Undefined
    d. Undefined

79. _____ are a set of equations containing multiple variables.
    a. Thing
    b. Systems of equations0
    c. Undefined
    d. Undefined

80. _____ are elementary linear transformations on a matrix which preserve matrix equivalence.
    a. Elementary row operations0
    b. Thing
    c. Undefined
    d. Undefined

81. Elementary _____ are simple transformations which can be applied to a matrix without changing the linear system of equations that it represents.
    a. Row operations0
    b. Thing
    c. Undefined
    d. Undefined

82. In linear algebra, the _____ of a matrix is obtained by combining two matrices in such a way that a matrix of coefficients to which has been added a column of constants corresponds to the right hand side of the equations.
    a. Augmented matrix0
    b. Thing
    c. Undefined
    d. Undefined

83. _____ is a fixed, but possibly unspecified, value. This is in contrast to a variable, which is not fixed.
    a. Thing
    b. Constant term0
    c. Undefined
    d. Undefined

84. A _____ is a compensation which workers receive in exchange for their labor.

Chapter 4. Matrices

a. Thing
b. Wage0
c. Undefined
d. Undefined

85. A _____ is a negotiable instrument instructing a financial institution to pay a specific amount of a specific currency from a specific demand account held in the maker/depositor's name with that institution. Both the maker and payee may be natural persons or legal entities.
   a. Check0
   b. Thing
   c. Undefined
   d. Undefined

86. In common philosophical language, a proposition or _____, is the content of an assertion, that is, it is true-or-false and defined by the meaning of a particular piece of language.
   a. Statement0
   b. Concept
   c. Undefined
   d. Undefined

87. _____ are the basic objects of study in graph theory. Informally speaking, a graph is a set of objects called points, nodes, or vertices connected by links called lines or edges.
   a. Graphs0
   b. Thing
   c. Undefined
   d. Undefined

88. In mathematics, the _____ of two sets A and B is the set that contains all elements of A that also belong to B (or equivalently, all elements of B that also belong to A), but no other elements.
   a. Thing
   b. Intersection0
   c. Undefined
   d. Undefined

89. _____ has one 90° internal angle a right angle.
   a. Right triangle0
   b. Thing
   c. Undefined
   d. Undefined

90. _____ is the application of tools and a processing medium to the transformation of raw materials into finished goods for sale.
   a. Thing
   b. Manufacturing0
   c. Undefined
   d. Undefined

91. _____ is the mathematical action of repeatedly adding or subtracting one, usually to find out how many objects there are or to set aside a desired number of objects.
   a. Thing
   b. Counting0
   c. Undefined
   d. Undefined

92. A _____ is a symbol or group of symbols, or a word in a natural language that represents a number.
   a. Numeral0
   b. Thing
   c. Undefined
   d. Undefined

93. The _____ of measurement are a globally standardized and modernized form of the metric system.
   a. Thing
   b. Units0
   c. Undefined
   d. Undefined

Chapter 4. Matrices

94. _____ mathematical functions take numeric arguments and produce numeric results.
   a. Thing
   b. Miscellaneous0
   c. Undefined
   d. Undefined

95. The mathematical concept of a _____ expresses the intuitive idea of deterministic dependence between two quantities, one of which is viewed as primary and the other as secondary. A _____ then is a way to associate a unique output for each input of a specified type, for example, a real number or an element of a given set.
   a. Function0
   b. Thing
   c. Undefined
   d. Undefined

96. A _____ defined function $f(x)$ of a real variable x is a function whose definition is given differently on disjoint subsets of its domain.
   a. Thing
   b. Piecewise0
   c. Undefined
   d. Undefined

97. _____, from Latin meaning "to make progress", is defined in two different ways. Pure economic _____ is the increase in wealth that an investor has from making an investment, taking into consideration all costs associated with that investment including the opportunity cost of capital.
   a. Thing
   b. Profit0
   c. Undefined
   d. Undefined

98. In set theory and its applications throughout mathematics, _____ are a collection of sets (or sometimes other mathematical objects) that can be unambiguously defined by a property that all its members share.
   a. Classes0
   b. Thing
   c. Undefined
   d. Undefined

99. In mathematics, a matrix is in row _____ if is satisfies the following requirements: • All nonzero rows are above any rows of all zeroes. • The leading coefficient of a row is always strictly to the right of the leading coefficient of the row above it.
   a. Echelon form0
   b. Thing
   c. Undefined
   d. Undefined

100. A _____ is a one-dimensional picture in which the integers are shown as specially-marked points evenly spaced on a line.
   a. Number line0
   b. Thing
   c. Undefined
   d. Undefined

101. In mathematics, a _____ is a condition that a solution to an optimization problem must satisfy in order to be acceptable.
   a. Constraint0
   b. Thing
   c. Undefined
   d. Undefined

102. In mathematics, a _____ is an ordered list of objects. Like a set, it contains members, also called elements or terms, and the number of terms is called the length of the _____. Unlike a set, order matters, and the exact same elements can appear multiple times at different positions in the _____.

a. Thing
c. Undefined

b. Sequence0
d. Undefined

Chapter 5. Quadratic Functions

1. A _____ is a polynomial function of the form $f(x) = ax^2 + bx + c$, where a, b, c are real numbers and $a \neq 0$.
   a. Quadratic function0
   b. Event
   c. Undefined
   d. Undefined

2. _____ is the design, analysis, and/or construction of works for practical purposes.
   a. Engineering0
   b. Thing
   c. Undefined
   d. Undefined

3. The mathematical concept of a _____ expresses the intuitive idea of deterministic dependence between two quantities, one of which is viewed as primary and the other as secondary. A _____ then is a way to associate a unique output for each input of a specified type, for example, a real number or an element of a given set.
   a. Thing
   b. Function0
   c. Undefined
   d. Undefined

4. In mathematics, a _____ is a polynomial equation of the second degree. The general form is $ax^2 + bx + c = 0$.
   a. Quadratic equation0
   b. Thing
   c. Undefined
   d. Undefined

5. A quadratic equation with real solutions, called roots, which may be real or complex, is given by the _____: $x = \frac{-b \pm \sqrt{b^2 - 4ac}}{2a}$.
   a. Thing
   b. Quadratic formula0
   c. Undefined
   d. Undefined

6. In plane geometry, a _____ is a polygon with four equal sides, four right angles, and parallel opposite sides. In algebra, the _____ of a number is that number multiplied by itself.
   a. Square0
   b. Thing
   c. Undefined
   d. Undefined

7. An _____ is a combination of numbers, operators, grouping symbols and/or free variables and bound variables arranged in a meaningful way which can be evaluated..
   a. Thing
   b. Expression0
   c. Undefined
   d. Undefined

8. In mathematics, _____ is the decomposition of an object into a product of other objects, or factors, which when multiplied together give the original.
   a. Factoring0
   b. Thing
   c. Undefined
   d. Undefined

9. _____ is a technique used in algebra to solve quadratic equations, in analytic geometry for determining the shapes of graphs, and in calculus for computing integrals, including, but hardly limited to, the integrals that define Laplace transforms. The essential objective is to reduce a quadratic polynomial in a variable in an equation or expression to a squared polynomial of linear order. This can reduce an equation or integral to one that is more easily solved or evaluated.
   a. Completing the square0
   b. Thing
   c. Undefined
   d. Undefined

Chapter 5. Quadratic Functions

10. A _____, as defined by the International Astronomical Union, is a celestial body orbiting a star or stellar remnant that is massive enough to be rounded by its own gravity, not massive enough to cause thermonuclear fusion in its core, and has cleared its neighboring region of planetesimals.
   a. Thing
   b. Planet0
   c. Undefined
   d. Undefined

11. _____ is defined as the rate of change or derivative with respect to time of velocity.
   a. Acceleration0
   b. Thing
   c. Undefined
   d. Undefined

12. The word _____ comes from the Latin word linearis, which means created by lines.
   a. Thing
   b. Linear0
   c. Undefined
   d. Undefined

13. In elementary algebra, a _____ is a polynomial with two terms: the sum of two monomials. It is the simplest kind of polynomial except for a monomial.
   a. Thing
   b. Binomial0
   c. Undefined
   d. Undefined

14. _____, Greek for "knowledge of nature," is the branch of science concerned with the discovery and characterization of universal laws which govern matter, energy, space, and time.
   a. Physics0
   b. Thing
   c. Undefined
   d. Undefined

15. A _____ is a unit of length, usually used to measure distance, in a number of different systems, including Imperial units, United States customary units and Norwegian/Swedish mil. Its size can vary from system to system, but in each is between 1 and 10 kilometers. In contemporary English contexts _____ refers to either:
   a. Thing
   b. Mile0
   c. Undefined
   d. Undefined

16. _____ is a unit of speed, expressing the number of international miles covered per hour.
   a. Thing
   b. Miles per hour0
   c. Undefined
   d. Undefined

17. A _____ is a first degree polynomial mathematical function of the form: f(x) = mx + b where m and b are real constants and x is a real variable.
   a. Thing
   b. Linear function0
   c. Undefined
   d. Undefined

18. _____ is often used to describe the measurement of the steepness, incline, gradient, or grade of a straight line. The _____ is defined as the ratio of the "rise" divided by the "run" between two points on a line, or in other words, the ratio of the altitude change to the horizontal distance between any two points on the line.
   a. Slope0
   b. Thing
   c. Undefined
   d. Undefined

19. In mathematics a _____ is a function which defines a distance between elements of a set.

a. Thing
b. Metric0
c. Undefined
d. Undefined

20. In mathematics, the _____ is a conic section generated by the intersection of a right circular conical surface and a plane parallel to a generating straight line of that surface. It can also be defined as locus of points in a plane which are equidistant from a given point.
   a. Parabola0
   b. Thing
   c. Undefined
   d. Undefined

21. _____ means "constancy", i.e. if something retains a certain feature even after we change a way of looking at it, then it is symmetric.
   a. Thing
   b. Symmetry0
   c. Undefined
   d. Undefined

22. An _____ is a straight line around which a geometric figure can be rotated.
   a. Axis0
   b. Thing
   c. Undefined
   d. Undefined

23. _____ of a two-dimensional figure is a line such that, if a perpendicular is constructed, any two points lying on the perpendicular at equal distances from the _____ are identical.
   a. Thing
   b. Axis of symmetry0
   c. Undefined
   d. Undefined

24. In mathematics, _____ is a part of the set theoretic notion of function.
   a. Thing
   b. Image0
   c. Undefined
   d. Undefined

25. In geometry, a _____ is a special kind of point, usually a corner of a polygon, polyhedron, or higher dimensional polytope. In the geometry of curves a _____ is a point of where the first derivative of curvature is zero. In graph theory, a _____ is the fundamental unit out of which graphs are formed
   a. Vertex0
   b. Thing
   c. Undefined
   d. Undefined

26. In mathematics, a _____ may be described informally as a number that can be given by an infinite decimal representation.
   a. Real number0
   b. Thing
   c. Undefined
   d. Undefined

27. In mathematics, a _____ of a k-place relation $L \subseteq X_1 \times \ldots \times X_k$ is one of the sets X_j, $1 \leq j \leq k$. In the special case where k = 2 and $L \subseteq X_1 \times X_2$ is a function $L : X_1 \to X_2$, it is conventional to refer to X_1 as the _____ of the function and to refer to X_2 as the codomain of the function.
   a. Thing
   b. Domain0
   c. Undefined
   d. Undefined

28. In mathematics, an inequality is a statement about the relative size or order of two objects. For example 14 > 10, or 14 is _____ 10.

Chapter 5. Quadratic Functions

    a. Thing
    c. Undefined
    b. Greater than0
    d. Undefined

29. In mathematics, the _____ of a function is the set of all "output" values produced by that function. Given a function $f : A \to B$, the _____ of f, is defined to be the set $\{x \in B : x = f(a) \text{ for some } a \in A\}$.
    a. Thing
    c. Undefined
    b. Range0
    d. Undefined

30. A _____ is a set of numbers that designate location in a given reference system, such as x,y in a planar _____ system or an x,y,z in a three-dimensional _____ system.
    a. Coordinate0
    c. Undefined
    b. Thing
    d. Undefined

31. In mathematics, a _____ is a constant multiplicative factor of a certain object. The object can be such things as a variable, a vector, a function, etc. For example, the _____ of $9x^2$ is 9.
    a. Coefficient0
    c. Undefined
    b. Thing
    d. Undefined

32. Compass and straightedge or ruler-and-compass _____ is the _____ of lengths or angles using only an idealized ruler and compass.
    a. Thing
    c. Undefined
    b. Construction0
    d. Undefined

33. _____ of an object is its speed in a particular direction.
    a. Velocity0
    c. Undefined
    b. Thing
    d. Undefined

34. Initial objects are also called _____, and terminal objects are also called final.
    a. Coterminal0
    c. Undefined
    b. Thing
    d. Undefined

35. _____ is a synonym for information.
    a. Thing
    c. Undefined
    b. Data0
    d. Undefined

36. A _____, scatter diagram or scatter graph is a chart that uses Cartesian coordinates to display values for two variables.
    a. Scatter plot0
    c. Undefined
    b. Thing
    d. Undefined

37. _____ is a relation in Euclidean geometry among the three sides of a right triangle.
    a. Thing
    c. Undefined
    b. Pythagorean Theorem0
    d. Undefined

38. In mathematics, a _____ is a statement that can be proved on the basis of explicitly stated or previously agreed assumptions.

Chapter 5. Quadratic Functions

a. Theorem0
b. Thing
c. Undefined
d. Undefined

39. In mathematics, a _____ of a number x is a number r such that r^2 = x, or in words, a number r whose square (the result of multiplying the number by itself) is x.
   a. Square root0
   b. Thing
   c. Undefined
   d. Undefined

40. In mathematics, a _____ of a complex-valued function f is a member x of the domain of f such that f(x) vanishes at x, that is, x : f (x) = 0.
   a. Thing
   b. Root0
   c. Undefined
   d. Undefined

41. The plus and _____ signs are mathematical symbols used to represent the notions of positive and negative as well as the operations of addition and subtraction.
   a. Minus0
   b. Thing
   c. Undefined
   d. Undefined

42. In mathematics, a _____ is the end result of a division problem. It can also be expressed as the number of times the divisor divides into the dividend.
   a. Thing
   b. Quotient0
   c. Undefined
   d. Undefined

43. A _____ is a negotiable instrument instructing a financial institution to pay a specific amount of a specific currency from a specific demand account held in the maker/depositor's name with that institution. Both the maker and payee may be natural persons or legal entities.
   a. Check0
   b. Thing
   c. Undefined
   d. Undefined

44. In mathematics, the _____ of two sets A and B is the set that contains all elements of A that also belong to B (or equivalently, all elements of B that also belong to A), but no other elements.
   a. Thing
   b. Intersection0
   c. Undefined
   d. Undefined

45. In mathematics, a _____ is the result of multiplying, or an expression that identifies factors to be multiplied.
   a. Thing
   b. Product0
   c. Undefined
   d. Undefined

46. _____ is a branch of mathematics concerning the study of structure, relation and quantity.
   a. Algebra0
   b. Concept
   c. Undefined
   d. Undefined

47. In mathematics, a _____ is an n-tuple with n being 3.
   a. Triple0
   b. Thing
   c. Undefined
   d. Undefined

Chapter 5. Quadratic Functions

48. A _____ is one of the basic shapes of geometry: a polygon with three vertices and three sides which are straight line segments.
   a. Triangle0
   b. Thing
   c. Undefined
   d. Undefined

49. In mathematics, the additive inverse, or _____ of a number n is the number that, when added to n, yields zero. The additive inverse of n is denoted −n. For example, 7 is −7, because 7 + (−7) = 0, and the additive inverse of −0.3 is 0.3, because −0.3 + 0.3 = 0.
   a. Thing
   b. Opposite0
   c. Undefined
   d. Undefined

50. _____ has one 90° internal angle a right angle.
   a. Thing
   b. Right triangle0
   c. Undefined
   d. Undefined

51. In mathematics, the _____ of a number n is the number that, when added to n, yields zero. The _____ of n is denoted −n. For example, 7 is −7, because 7 + (−7) = 0, and the _____ of −0.3 is 0.3, because −0.3 + 0.3 = 0.
   a. Additive inverse0
   b. Thing
   c. Undefined
   d. Undefined

52. The _____ of measurement are a globally standardized and modernized form of the metric system.
   a. Thing
   b. Units0
   c. Undefined
   d. Undefined

53. The metre (or _____, see spelling differences) is a measure of length. It is the basic unit of length in the metric system and in the International System of Units (SI), used around the world for general and scientific purposes.
   a. Concept
   b. Meter0
   c. Undefined
   d. Undefined

54. In Euclidean geometry, a _____ is the set of all points in a plane at a fixed distance, called the radius, from a given point, the center.
   a. Thing
   b. Circle0
   c. Undefined
   d. Undefined

55. A _____ is a three-dimensional solid object bounded by six square faces, facets, or sides, with three meeting at each vertex.
   a. Thing
   b. Cube0
   c. Undefined
   d. Undefined

56. A _____ is a function that assigns a number to subsets of a given set.
   a. Thing
   b. Measure0
   c. Undefined
   d. Undefined

57. A _____ can refer to a line joining two nonadjacent vertices of a polygon or polyhedron, or in some contexts any upward or downward sloping line. .

Chapter 5. Quadratic Functions

a. Diagonal0
b. Thing
c. Undefined
d. Undefined

58. An n-sided _____ is a polyhedron formed by connecting an n-sided polygonal base and a point, called the apex, by n triangular faces. In other words, it is a conic solid with polygonal base.
    a. Pyramid0
    b. Thing
    c. Undefined
    d. Undefined

59. The _____ of a right circular cone is the distance from any point on the circle to the apex of the cone.
    a. Slant height0
    b. Thing
    c. Undefined
    d. Undefined

60. A _____ surface is the surface or face of a solid on its sides. It can also be defined as any face or surface that is not a base.
    a. Thing
    b. Lateral0
    c. Undefined
    d. Undefined

61. _____ are activities that are governed by a set of rules or customs and often engaged in competitively.
    a. Sports0
    b. Thing
    c. Undefined
    d. Undefined

62. _____ is the process of planning, recording, and controlling the movement of a craft or vehicle from one place to another.
    a. Navigation0
    b. Thing
    c. Undefined
    d. Undefined

63. In botany, _____ are above-ground plant organs specialized for photosynthesis. Their characteristics are typically analyzed by using Fiobonacci's sequences.
    a. Thing
    b. Leaves0
    c. Undefined
    d. Undefined

64. In geometry, the _____ of an object is a point in some sense in the middle of the object.
    a. Center0
    b. Thing
    c. Undefined
    d. Undefined

65. In mathematics, a _____ in elementary terms is any of a variety of different functions from geometry, such as rotations, reflections and translations.
    a. Transformation0
    b. Thing
    c. Undefined
    d. Undefined

66. _____ are the basic objects of study in graph theory. Informally speaking, a graph is a set of objects called points, nodes, or vertices connected by links called lines or edges.
    a. Thing
    b. Graphs0
    c. Undefined
    d. Undefined

67. _____ are of a number n in its third power-the result of multiplying it by itself three times.

Chapter 5. Quadratic Functions

    a. Cubes0
    b. Thing
    c. Undefined
    d. Undefined

68. _____ is the art and science of designing buildings and structures.
    a. Thing
    b. Architecture0
    c. Undefined
    d. Undefined

69. A _____ is the result of the addition of a set of numbers. The numbers may be natural numbers, complex numbers, matrices, or still more complicated objects. An infinite _____ is a subtle procedure known as a series.
    a. Thing
    b. Sum0
    c. Undefined
    d. Undefined

70. In mathematics, factorization (British English: factorisation) or factoring is the decomposition of an object (for example, a number, a polynomial, or a matrix) into a product of other objects, or _____, which when multiplied together give the original.
    a. Factors0
    b. Thing
    c. Undefined
    d. Undefined

71. A _____ is a polynomial consisting of three terms; in other words, it is the sum of three monomials.
    a. Thing
    b. Trinomial0
    c. Undefined
    d. Undefined

72. In mathematics and the mathematical sciences, a _____ is a fixed, but possibly unspecified, value. This is in contrast to a variable, which is not fixed.
    a. Thing
    b. Constant0
    c. Undefined
    d. Undefined

73. The _____ are the only integral domain whose positive elements are well-ordered, and in which order is preserved by addition. Like the natural numbers, the _____ form a countably infinite set. The set of all _____ is usually denoted in mathematics by a boldface Z .
    a. Integers0
    b. Thing
    c. Undefined
    d. Undefined

74. Acid _____ ratio measures the ability of a company to use its near cash or quick assets to immediately extinguish its current liabilities.
    a. Test0
    b. Thing
    c. Undefined
    d. Undefined

75. In mathematics the _____ refers to the identity: $a^2 - b^2 = (a+b)(a-b)$
    a. Difference of two squares0
    b. Thing
    c. Undefined
    d. Undefined

76. _____ is a notation for writing numbers that is often used by scientists and mathematicians to make it easier to write large and small numbers.

Chapter 5. Quadratic Functions

a. Thing
b. Scientific notation0
c. Undefined
d. Undefined

77. In geometry, a line _____ is a part of a line that is bounded by two end points, and contains every point on the line between its end points.
    a. Segment0
    b. Concept
    c. Undefined
    d. Undefined

78. A _____ is a part of a line that is bounded by two end points, and contains every point on the line between its end points.
    a. Thing
    b. Line segment0
    c. Undefined
    d. Undefined

79. In geometry, an _____ of a triangle is a straight line through a vertex and perpendicular to (i.e. forming a right angle with) the opposite side or an extension of the opposite side.
    a. Concept
    b. Altitude0
    c. Undefined
    d. Undefined

80. In classical geometry, a _____ of a circle or sphere is any line segment from its center to its boundary. By extension, the _____ of a circle or sphere is the length of any such segment. The _____ is half the diameter. In science and engineering the term _____ of curvature is commonly used as a synonym for _____.
    a. Thing
    b. Radius0
    c. Undefined
    d. Undefined

81. The _____ of a right triangle is the triangle's longest side; the side opposite the right angle.
    a. Thing
    b. Hypotenuse0
    c. Undefined
    d. Undefined

82. A _____ is a one-dimensional picture in which the integers are shown as specially-marked points evenly spaced on a line.
    a. Thing
    b. Number line0
    c. Undefined
    d. Undefined

83. In mathematics, an _____ is a statement about the relative size or order of two objects.
    a. Thing
    b. Inequality0
    c. Undefined
    d. Undefined

84. In mathematics, the concept of a _____ tries to capture the intuitive idea of a geometrical one-dimensional and continuous object. A simple example is the circle.
    a. Curve0
    b. Thing
    c. Undefined
    d. Undefined

85. _____ is the shape of a hanging flexible chain or cable when supported at its ends and acted upon by a uniform gravitational force. The chain is steepest near the points of suspension because this part of the chain has the most weight pulling down on it. Toward the bottom, the slope of the chain decreases because the chain is supporting less weight.

Chapter 5. Quadratic Functions

    a. Catenary0
    b. Thing
    c. Undefined
    d. Undefined

86. In physics, _____ is an influence that may cause an object to accelerate. It may be experienced as a lift, a push, or a pull. The actual acceleration of the body is determined by the vector sum of all forces acting on it, known as net _____ or resultant _____.
    a. Thing
    b. Force0
    c. Undefined
    d. Undefined

87. The term _____ can refer to an integer which is the square of some other integer, or an algebraic expression that can be factored as the square of some other expression.
    a. Perfect square0
    b. Thing
    c. Undefined
    d. Undefined

88. _____ is a fixed, but possibly unspecified, value. This is in contrast to a variable, which is not fixed.
    a. Thing
    b. Constant term0
    c. Undefined
    d. Undefined

89. In Euclidean geometry, a _____ is moving every point a constant distance in a specified direction.
    a. Translation0
    b. Concept
    c. Undefined
    d. Undefined

90. In astronomy, geography, geometry and related sciences and contexts, a plane is said to be _____ at a given point if it is locally perpendicular to the gradient of the gravity field, i.e., with the direction of the gravitational force at that point.
    a. Thing
    b. Horizontal0
    c. Undefined
    d. Undefined

91. In geometry, a _____ is defined as a quadrilateral where all four of its angles are right angles.
    a. Thing
    b. Rectangle0
    c. Undefined
    d. Undefined

92. _____ has many meanings, most of which simply .
    a. Power0
    b. Thing
    c. Undefined
    d. Undefined

93. _____, from Latin meaning "to make progress", is defined in two different ways. Pure economic _____ is the increase in wealth that an investor has from making an investment, taking into consideration all costs associated with that investment including the opportunity cost of capital.
    a. Profit0
    b. Thing
    c. Undefined
    d. Undefined

94. An _____ is a collection of two not necessarily distinct objects, one of which is distinguished as the first coordinate and the other as the second coordinate.
    a. Ordered pair0
    b. Thing
    c. Undefined
    d. Undefined

Chapter 5. Quadratic Functions

95. In mathematics, the conjugate _____ or adjoint matrix of an m-by-n matrix A with complex entries is the n-by-m matrix A* obtained from A by taking the transpose and then taking the complex conjugate of each entry.
    a. Pairs0
    b. Thing
    c. Undefined
    d. Undefined

96. In mathematics, an _____ number is any real number that is not a rational number- that is, it is a number which cannot be expressed as a fraction m/n, where m and n are integers.
    a. Thing
    b. Irrational0
    c. Undefined
    d. Undefined

97. In mathematics, an _____ is any real number that is not a rational number ¡ª that is, it is a number which cannot be expressed as m/n, where m and n are integers.
    a. Irrational number0
    b. Thing
    c. Undefined
    d. Undefined

98. In mathematics, _____ are any real number that is not a rational number ¡ª that is, it is a number which cannot be expressed as m/n, where m and n are integers.
    a. Irrational numbers0
    b. Thing
    c. Undefined
    d. Undefined

99. _____ forms part of thinking. Considered the most complex of all intellectual functions, _____ has been defined as higher-order cognitive process that requires the modulation and control of more routine or fundamental skills.
    a. Thing
    b. Problem solving0
    c. Undefined
    d. Undefined

100. The deductive-nomological model is a formalized view of scientific _____ in natural language.
    a. Explanation0
    b. Thing
    c. Undefined
    d. Undefined

101. In mathematics, an _____, mean, or central tendency of a data set refers to a measure of the "middle" or "expected" value of the data set.
    a. Concept
    b. Average0
    c. Undefined
    d. Undefined

102. In mathematics, the multiplicative inverse of a number x, denoted 1/x or x^{-1}, is the number which, when multiplied by x, yields 1. The multiplicative inverse of x is also called the _____ of x.
    a. Reciprocal0
    b. Thing
    c. Undefined
    d. Undefined

103. In geometry, a _____ is the intersection of a body in 2-dimensional space with a line, or of a body in 3-dimensional space with a plane
    a. Cross section0
    b. Thing
    c. Undefined
    d. Undefined

104. Multiple Signal Classification, also known as _____, is an algorithm used for frequency estimation and emitter location.

Chapter 5. Quadratic Functions

a. Thing
c. Undefined

b. Music0
d. Undefined

105. A _____ is an individual or household that purchases and uses goods and services generated within the economy.
 a. Thing
 c. Undefined

 b. Consumer0
 d. Undefined

106. In economics, supply and _____ describe market relations between prospective sellers and buyers of a good.
 a. Thing
 c. Undefined

 b. Demand0
 d. Undefined

107. A _____ signifies a point or points of probability on a subject e.g., the _____ of creativity, which allows for the formation of rule or norm or law by interpretation of the phenomena events that can be created.
 a. Principle0
 c. Undefined

 b. Thing
 d. Undefined

108. The _____ is a number often encountered when taking the ratios of distances in simple geometric figures. It is approximately 1.6180339887.
 a. Golden ratio0
 c. Undefined

 b. Thing
 d. Undefined

109. A _____ is a quantity that denotes the proportional amount or magnitude of one quantity relative to another.
 a. Ratio0
 c. Undefined

 b. Thing
 d. Undefined

110. The _____, the average in everyday English, which is also called the arithmetic _____ (and is distinguished from the geometric _____ or harmonic _____). The average is also called the sample _____. The expected value of a random variable, which is also called the population _____.
 a. Mean0
 c. Undefined

 b. Thing
 d. Undefined

111. In mathematics, a _____ is a rectangular table of numbers or, more generally, a table consisting of abstract quantities that can be added and multiplied.
 a. Thing
 c. Undefined

 b. Matrix0
 d. Undefined

112. _____ element of an element x with respect to a binary operation * with identity element e is an element y such that x * y = y * x = e. In particular,
 a. Thing
 c. Undefined

 b. Inverse0
 d. Undefined

113. In mathematics, a _____ is a number in the form of a + bi where a and b are real numbers, and i is the imaginary unit, with the property i 2 = −1. The real number a is called the real part of the _____, and the real number b is the imaginary part.

Chapter 5. Quadratic Functions

    a. Thing
    b. Complex number0
    c. Undefined
    d. Undefined

114. In business, particularly accounting, a _____ is the time intervals that the accounts, statement, payments, or other calculations cover.
    a. Period0
    b. Thing
    c. Undefined
    d. Undefined

115. A _____ is a simplified and structured visual representation of concepts, ideas, constructions, relations, statistical data, anatomy etc used in all aspects of human activities to visualize and clarify the topic.
    a. Thing
    b. Diagram0
    c. Undefined
    d. Undefined

116. _____ is the property of a physical object that quantifies the amount of matter and energy it is equivalent to.
    a. Thing
    b. Mass0
    c. Undefined
    d. Undefined

117. In mathematics, defined and _____ are used to explain whether or not expressions have meaningful, sensible, and unambiguous values.
    a. Undefined0
    b. Thing
    c. Undefined
    d. Undefined

118. _____ is the symbold used to indicate the nth root of a number
    a. Thing
    b. Radical0
    c. Undefined
    d. Undefined

119. Leonhard _____ was a pioneering Swiss mathematician and physicist, who spent most of his life in Russia and Germany.
    a. Person
    b. Euler0
    c. Undefined
    d. Undefined

120. In mathematics, an _____ number is a complex number whose square is a negative real number. They were defined in 1572 by Rafael Bombelli.
    a. Thing
    b. Imaginary0
    c. Undefined
    d. Undefined

121. In mathematics, the _____ i (or sometimes the Latin j or the Greek iota, see below) allows the real number system R to be extended to the complex number system C. Its precise definition is dependent upon the particular method of extension.
    a. Imaginary unit0
    b. Thing
    c. Undefined
    d. Undefined

122. _____ was a pioneering Swiss mathematician and physicist, who spent most of his life in Russia and Germany.

Chapter 5. Quadratic Functions

    a. Leonhard Euler0
    c. Undefined
    b. Person
    d. Undefined

123. In mathematics, the word _____ is used informally to refer to certain distinct bodies of knowledge about mathematics.
    a. Theoretical0
    b. Thing
    c. Undefined
    d. Undefined

124. In mathematics, an _____ is a complex number whose square is a negative real number. They were defined in 1572 by Rafael Bombelli.
    a. Imaginary number0
    b. Thing
    c. Undefined
    d. Undefined

125. In mathematics, the _____ of a complex number z, is the first element of the ordered pair of real numbers representing z, i.e. if z = (x,y), or equivalently, z = x + iy, then the _____ of z is x. It is denoted by Re{z} . The complex function which maps z to the _____ of z is not holomorphic.
    a. Thing
    b. Real part0
    c. Undefined
    d. Undefined

126. In mathematics, the _____ of a complex number z, is the second element of the ordered pair of real numbers representing z, i.e. if z = (x,y), or equivalently, z = x + iy, then the _____ of z is y.
    a. Imaginary part0
    b. Thing
    c. Undefined
    d. Undefined

127. In mathematics, the _____ inverse, or opposite, of a number n is the number that, when added to n, yields zero. The _____ inverse of n is denoted −n.
    a. Additive0
    b. Thing
    c. Undefined
    d. Undefined

128. In mathematics, and in particular in abstract algebra, the _____ is a property of binary operations that generalises the distributive law from elementary algebra.
    a. Distributive property0
    b. Thing
    c. Undefined
    d. Undefined

129. In algebra, a _____ is a binomial formed by taking the opposite of the second term of a binomial.
    a. Conjugate0
    b. Thing
    c. Undefined
    d. Undefined

130. A _____ is the part of a fraction that tells how many equal parts make up a whole, and which is used in the name of the fraction: "halves", "thirds", "fourths" or "quarters", "fifths" and so on.
    a. Concept
    b. Denominator0
    c. Undefined
    d. Undefined

131. In statistics, _____ means the most frequent value assumed by a random variable, or occurring in a sampling of a random variable.

a. Mode0
b. Concept
c. Undefined
d. Undefined

132. In mathematics, a _____ is a two-dimensional manifold or surface that is perfectly flat.
   a. Thing
   b. Plane0
   c. Undefined
   d. Undefined

133. In mathematics, the _____ (or modulus) of a real number is its numerical value without regard to its sign.
   a. Absolute value0
   b. Thing
   c. Undefined
   d. Undefined

134. In mathematics, a _____ (also spelled reflexion) is a map that transforms an object into its mirror image.
   a. Concept
   b. Reflection0
   c. Undefined
   d. Undefined

135. A _____ is a movement of an object in a circular motion. A two-dimensional object rotates around a center (or point) of _____. A three-dimensional object rotates around a line called an axis. If the axis of _____ is within the body, the body is said to rotate upon itself, or spin—which implies relative speed and perhaps free-movement with angular momentum. A circular motion about an external point, e.g. the Earth about the Sun, is called an orbit or more properly an orbital revolution.
   a. Rotation0
   b. Thing
   c. Undefined
   d. Undefined

136. _____ is finding a curve which matches a series of data points and possibly other constraints.
   a. Curve fitting0
   b. Thing
   c. Undefined
   d. Undefined

137. A _____ is a symbolic representation denoting a quantity or expression. It often represents an "unknown" quantity that has the potential to change.
   a. Thing
   b. Variable0
   c. Undefined
   d. Undefined

138. A _____ is an equation in which each term is either a constant or the product of a constant times the first power of a variable.
   a. Linear equation0
   b. Thing
   c. Undefined
   d. Undefined

139. In geographic information systems, a _____ comprises an entity with a geographic location, typically determined by points, arcs, or polygons. Carriageways and cadastres exemplify _____ data.
   a. Thing
   b. Feature0
   c. Undefined
   d. Undefined

140. In algebra, a _____ is a function depending on n that associates a scalar, det(A), to every $n \times n$ square matrix A.
   a. Determinant0
   b. Thing
   c. Undefined
   d. Undefined

Chapter 5. Quadratic Functions

141. _____ is a business term for the amount of money that a company receives from its activities in a given period, mostly from sales of products and/or services to customers
   a. Thing
   b. Revenue0
   c. Undefined
   d. Undefined

142. In elementary algebra, an _____ is a set that contains every real number between two indicated numbers and may contain the two numbers themselves.
   a. Thing
   b. Interval0
   c. Undefined
   d. Undefined

143. In mathematics, _____ geometry was the traditional name for the geometry of three-dimensional Euclidean space — for practical purposes the kind of space we live in.
   a. Thing
   b. Solid0
   c. Undefined
   d. Undefined

144. _____, or Rationalisation in mathematics is the process of removing a square root or imaginary number from the denominator of a fraction.
   a. Thing
   b. Rationalizing0
   c. Undefined
   d. Undefined

145. _____ of a polynomial with real or complex coefficients is a certain expression in the coefficients of the polynomial which is equal to zero if and only if the polynomial has a multiple root i.e. a root with multiplicity greater than one in the complex numbers.
   a. Thing
   b. Discriminant0
   c. Undefined
   d. Undefined

146. In mathematics, a _____ is an algebraic structure in which addition and multiplication are defined and have properties listed below.
   a. Ring0
   b. Thing
   c. Undefined
   d. Undefined

147. In mathematics, the _____ f is the collection of all ordered pairs . In particular, graph means the graphical representation of this collection, in the form of a curve or surface, together with axes, etc. Graphing on a Cartesian plane is sometimes referred to as curve sketching.
   a. Thing
   b. Graph of a function0
   c. Undefined
   d. Undefined

148. _____ is a term applied when talking about the movement of air from one place to the next.
   a. Thing
   b. Wind speed0
   c. Undefined
   d. Undefined

149. _____ are external two-dimensional outlines, with the appearance or configuration of some thing - in contrast to the matter or content or substance of which it is composed.
   a. Thing
   b. Shapes0
   c. Undefined
   d. Undefined

150. In mathematics, a _____ is a condition that a solution to an optimization problem must satisfy in order to be acceptable.
   a. Constraint0
   b. Thing
   c. Undefined
   d. Undefined

151. In mathematics, a _____ is an ordered list of objects. Like a set, it contains members, also called elements or terms, and the number of terms is called the length of the _____. Unlike a set, order matters, and the exact same elements can appear multiple times at different positions in the _____.
   a. Sequence0
   b. Thing
   c. Undefined
   d. Undefined

Chapter 6. Exponential and Logarirhmic Functions

1. In mathematics, the _____ is the logarithm with base 10.
   a. Thing
   b. Common logarithm0
   c. Undefined
   d. Undefined

2. In mathematics, _____ growth occurs when the growth rate of a function is always proportional to the function's current size.
   a. Exponential0
   b. Thing
   c. Undefined
   d. Undefined

3. _____ is one of the most important functions in mathematics. A function commonly used to study growth and decay
   a. Exponential function0
   b. Thing
   c. Undefined
   d. Undefined

4. In mathematics, _____ occurs when the growth rate of a function is always proportional to the function's current size.
   a. Exponential growth0
   b. Thing
   c. Undefined
   d. Undefined

5. In mathematics, a _____ of a number x is the exponent y of the power by such that $x = b^y$. The value used for the base b must be neither 0 nor 1, nor a root of 1 in the case of the extension to complex numbers, and is typically 10, e, or 2.
   a. Thing
   b. Logarithm0
   c. Undefined
   d. Undefined

6. The mathematical concept of a _____ expresses the intuitive idea of deterministic dependence between two quantities, one of which is viewed as primary and the other as secondary. A _____ then is a way to associate a unique output for each input of a specified type, for example, a real number or an element of a given set.
   a. Thing
   b. Function0
   c. Undefined
   d. Undefined

7. _____ is the process in which an unstable atomic nucleus loses energy by emitting radiation in the form of particles or electromagnetic waves.
   a. Radioactive decay0
   b. Thing
   c. Undefined
   d. Undefined

8. _____ is the fee paid on borrowed money.
   a. Thing
   b. Interest0
   c. Undefined
   d. Undefined

9. In sociology and biology a _____ is the collection of people or organisms of a particular species living in a given geographic area or space, usually measured by a census.
   a. Population0
   b. Thing
   c. Undefined
   d. Undefined

10. _____ is change in population over time, and can be quantified as the change in the number of individuals in a population per unit time.

a. Thing
b. Population growth0
c. Undefined
d. Undefined

11. _____ interest refers to the fact that whenever interest is calculated, it is based not only on the original principal, but also on any unpaid interest that has been added to the principal.
   a. Compound0
   b. Thing
   c. Undefined
   d. Undefined

12. _____ refers to the fact that whenever interest is calculated, it is based not only on the original principal, but also on any unpaid interest that has been added to the principal. The more frequently interest is compounded, the faster the balance grows.
   a. Compound interest0
   b. Concept
   c. Undefined
   d. Undefined

13. Sir Isaac _____, was an English physicist, mathematician, astronomer, natural philosopher, and alchemist, regarded by many as the greatest figure in the history of science
   a. Newton0
   b. Person
   c. Undefined
   d. Undefined

14. The _____, i.e., acoustic intensity is defined as the sound power P_{ac} per unit area A.
   a. Sound intensity0
   b. Thing
   c. Undefined
   d. Undefined

15. In Euclidean geometry, a uniform _____ is a linear transformation that enlargers or diminishes objects, and whose _____ factor is the same in all directions. This is also called homothethy.
   a. Thing
   b. Scale0
   c. Undefined
   d. Undefined

16. _____ is a physical property of a system that underlies the common notions of hot and cold; something that is hotter has the greater _____.
   a. Thing
   b. Temperature0
   c. Undefined
   d. Undefined

17. A _____ is a statement or claimt that a particular event will occur in the future in more certain terms than a forecast.
   a. Thing
   b. Prediction0
   c. Undefined
   d. Undefined

18. In mathematics and the mathematical sciences, a _____ is a fixed, but possibly unspecified, value. This is in contrast to a variable, which is not fixed.
   a. Thing
   b. Constant0
   c. Undefined
   d. Undefined

19. An _____ is a combination of numbers, operators, grouping symbols and/or free variables and bound variables arranged in a meaningful way which can be evaluated..

Chapter 6. Exponential and Logarirhmic Functions

    a. Thing   b. Expression0
    c. Undefined   d. Undefined

20. Initial objects are also called _____, and terminal objects are also called final.
    a. Thing   b. Coterminal0
    c. Undefined   d. Undefined

21. _____ is a synonym for information.
    a. Data0   b. Thing
    c. Undefined   d. Undefined

22. The _____ (symbol _____) and the millibar (symbol mbar, also mb) are units of pressure.
    a. Bar0   b. Thing
    c. Undefined   d. Undefined

23. _____ refers to selected population characteristics as used in government, marketing or opinion research, or the demographic profiles used in such research.
    a. Demographics0   b. Thing
    c. Undefined   d. Undefined

24. A _____ is a special kind of ratio, indicating a relationship between two measurements with different units, such as miles to gallons or cents to pounds.
    a. Thing   b. Rate0
    c. Undefined   d. Undefined

25. _____ is a kind of property which exists as magnitude or multitude. It is among the basic classes of things along with quality, substance, change, and relation.
    a. Thing   b. Amount0
    c. Undefined   d. Undefined

26. _____ is a decrease that follows an exponential function.
    a. Exponential decay0   b. Thing
    c. Undefined   d. Undefined

27. _____ are a measure of time.
    a. Minutes0   b. Thing
    c. Undefined   d. Undefined

28. In mathematics, a _____ is an n-tuple with n being 3.
    a. Thing   b. Triple0
    c. Undefined   d. Undefined

29. _____ is the level of functional and/or metabolic efficiency of an organism at both the micro level.
    a. Thing   b. Health0
    c. Undefined   d. Undefined

Chapter 6. Exponential and Logarirhmic Functions

30. _____ is electromagnetic radiation with a wavelength that is visible to the eye (visible _____) or, in a technical or scientific context, electromagnetic radiation of any wavelength.
   a. Light0
   b. Thing
   c. Undefined
   d. Undefined

31. _____ is a subset of a population.
   a. Sample0
   b. Thing
   c. Undefined
   d. Undefined

32. In chemistry, a _____ is substance made by combining two or more different materials in such a way that no chemical reaction occurs.
   a. Mixture0
   b. Thing
   c. Undefined
   d. Undefined

33. _____ is a set, with some particular properties and usually some additional structure, such as the operations of addition or multiplication, for instance.
   a. Thing
   b. Space0
   c. Undefined
   d. Undefined

34. A _____ is a vehicle, missile or aircraft which obtains thrust by the reaction to the ejection of fast moving fluid from within a _____ engine.
   a. Thing
   b. Rocket0
   c. Undefined
   d. Undefined

35. U.S. liquid _____ is legally defined as 231 cubic inches, and is equal to 3.785411784 litres or abotu 0.13368 cubic feet. This is the most common definition of a _____. The U.S. fluid ounce is defined as 1/128 of a U.S. _____.
   a. Thing
   b. Gallon0
   c. Undefined
   d. Undefined

36. A _____ is a symbolic representation denoting a quantity or expression. It often represents an "unknown" quantity that has the potential to change.
   a. Variable0
   b. Thing
   c. Undefined
   d. Undefined

37. In mathematics, a _____ in elementary terms is any of a variety of different functions from geometry, such as rotations, reflections and translations.
   a. Transformation0
   b. Thing
   c. Undefined
   d. Undefined

38. In geometry, a _____ is a special kind of point, usually a corner of a polygon, polyhedron, or higher dimensional polytope. In the geometry of curves a _____ is a point of where the first derivative of curvature is zero. In graph theory, a _____ is the fundamental unit out of which graphs are formed
   a. Thing
   b. Vertex0
   c. Undefined
   d. Undefined

Chapter 6. Exponential and Logarithmic Functions

39. In mathematics, the _____ is a conic section generated by the intersection of a right circular conical surface and a plane parallel to a generating straight line of that surface. It can also be defined as locus of points in a plane which are equidistant from a given point.
   a. Parabola0
   b. Thing
   c. Undefined
   d. Undefined

40. In elementary algebra, an _____ is a set that contains every real number between two indicated numbers and may contain the two numbers themselves.
   a. Interval0
   b. Thing
   c. Undefined
   d. Undefined

41. In geographic information systems, a _____ comprises an entity with a geographic location, typically determined by points, arcs, or polygons. Carriageways and cadastres exemplify _____ data.
   a. Thing
   b. Feature0
   c. Undefined
   d. Undefined

42. The word _____ comes from the Latin word linearis, which means created by lines.
   a. Linear0
   b. Thing
   c. Undefined
   d. Undefined

43. A _____ is a first degree polynomial mathematical function of the form: f(x) = mx + b where m and b are real constants and x is a real variable.
   a. Thing
   b. Linear function0
   c. Undefined
   d. Undefined

44. _____ is a regression method that models the relationship between a dependent variable Y, independent variables Xp, and a random term å.
   a. Thing
   b. Linear regression0
   c. Undefined
   d. Undefined

45. _____ or investing is a term with several closely-related meanings in business management, finance and economics, related to saving or deferring consumption.
   a. Thing
   b. Investment0
   c. Undefined
   d. Undefined

46. In mathematics, a _____ may be described informally as a number that can be given by an infinite decimal representation.
   a. Thing
   b. Real number0
   c. Undefined
   d. Undefined

47. An _____ is a straight line or curve A to which another curve B approaches closer and closer as one moves along it. As one moves along B, the space between it and the _____ A becomes smaller and smaller, and can in fact be made as small as one could wish by going far enough along. A curve may or may not touch or cross its _____. In fact, the curve may intersect the _____ an infinite number of times.

Chapter 6. Exponential and Logarirhmic Functions

    a. Thing
    b. Asymptote0
    c. Undefined
    d. Undefined

48. _____ are the basic objects of study in graph theory. Informally speaking, a graph is a set of objects called points, nodes, or vertices connected by links called lines or edges.
    a. Graphs0
    b. Thing
    c. Undefined
    d. Undefined

49. In mathematics, a _____ (also spelled reflexion) is a map that transforms an object into its mirror image.
    a. Reflection0
    b. Concept
    c. Undefined
    d. Undefined

50. Any point where a graph makes contact with an coordinate axis is called an _____ of the graph
    a. Thing
    b. Intercept0
    c. Undefined
    d. Undefined

51. In mathematics, the _____ of a function is the set of all "output" values produced by that function. Given a function $f : A \to B$, the _____ of f, is defined to be the set $\{x \in B : x = f(a) \text{ for some } a \in A\}$.
    a. Range0
    b. Thing
    c. Undefined
    d. Undefined

52. In mathematics, a _____ of a k-place relation $L \subseteq X_1 \times \ldots \times X_k$ is one of the sets X_j, $1 \le j \le k$. In the special case where k = 2 and $L \subseteq X_1 \times X_2$ is a function $L : X_1 \to X_2$, it is conventional to refer to X_1 as the _____ of the function and to refer to X_2 as the codomain of the function.
    a. Thing
    b. Domain0
    c. Undefined
    d. Undefined

53. An _____ is the fee paid on borrow money.
    a. Concept
    b. Interest rate0
    c. Undefined
    d. Undefined

54. In business, particularly accounting, a _____ is the time intervals that the accounts, statement, payments, or other calculations cover.
    a. Period0
    b. Thing
    c. Undefined
    d. Undefined

55. In astronomy, geography, geometry and related sciences and contexts, a plane is said to be _____ at a given point if it is locally perpendicular to the gradient of the gravity field, i.e., with the direction of the gravitational force at that point.
    a. Thing
    b. Horizontal0
    c. Undefined
    d. Undefined

56. _____ is a mathematical science pertaining to the collection, analysis, interpretation or explanation, and presentation of data. It is applicable to a wide variety of academic disciplines, from the physical and social sciences to the humanities.

Chapter 6. Exponential and Logarirhmic Functions

  a. Statistics0   b. Thing
  c. Undefined   d. Undefined

57. A _____ is a form of collective investment that pools money from many investors and invests their money in stocks, bonds, short-term money market instruments, and/or other securities.
  a. Mutual fund0   b. Thing
  c. Undefined   d. Undefined

58. In mainstream economics, the word _____ refers to a general rise in prices measured against a standard level of purchasing power.
  a. Thing   b. Inflation0
  c. Undefined   d. Undefined

59. _____ is a way of expressing a number as a fraction of 100 per cent meaning "per hundred".
  a. Percent0   b. Thing
  c. Undefined   d. Undefined

60. A _____ or CD is a time deposit, a financial product commonly offered to consumers by banks, thrift institutions, and credit unions.
  a. Thing   b. Certificate of deposit0
  c. Undefined   d. Undefined

61. A _____ defined function $f(x)$ of a real variable x is a function whose definition is given differently on disjoint subsets of its domain.
  a. Piecewise0   b. Thing
  c. Undefined   d. Undefined

62. In mathematics, a _____ is the result of multiplying, or an expression that identifies factors to be multiplied.
  a. Thing   b. Product0
  c. Undefined   d. Undefined

63. In mathematics, a _____ is a rectangular table of numbers or, more generally, a table consisting of abstract quantities that can be added and multiplied.
  a. Thing   b. Matrix0
  c. Undefined   d. Undefined

64. A _____ is a polynomial function of the form $f(x) = ax^2 + bx + c$, where a, b, c are real numbers and a , 0.
  a. Quadratic function0   b. Event
  c. Undefined   d. Undefined

65. Equivalence is the condition of being _____ or essentially equal.
  a. Equivalent0   b. Thing
  c. Undefined   d. Undefined

66. A _____ is 360° or 2δ radians.

Chapter 6. Exponential and Logarirhmic Functions

    a. Thing
    b. Turn0
    c. Undefined
    d. Undefined

67. In mathematics, an inequality is a statement about the relative size or order of two objects. For example 14 > 10, or 14 is _____ 10.
    a. Greater than0
    b. Thing
    c. Undefined
    d. Undefined

68. _____ is a mathematical operation, written a^n, involving two numbers, the base a and the exponent n.
    a. Exponentiating0
    b. Thing
    c. Undefined
    d. Undefined

69. _____ is a mathematical operation, written a^n, involving two numbers, the base a and the exponent n.
    a. Thing
    b. Exponentiation0
    c. Undefined
    d. Undefined

70. The _____ relative to a specified or implied reference level.
    a. Thing
    b. Decibel0
    c. Undefined
    d. Undefined

71. _____ is the estimation of a physical quantity such as distance, energy, temperature, or time.
    a. Thing
    b. Measurement0
    c. Undefined
    d. Undefined

72. _____ element of an element x with respect to a binary operation * with identity element e is an element y such that x * y = y * x = e. In particular,
    a. Inverse0
    b. Thing
    c. Undefined
    d. Undefined

73. A _____ is a function that assigns a number to subsets of a given set.
    a. Thing
    b. Measure0
    c. Undefined
    d. Undefined

74. _____ is a measure of the acidity or alkalinity of a solution.
    a. Thing
    b. PH level0
    c. Undefined
    d. Undefined

75. A _____ is a negotiable instrument instructing a financial institution to pay a specific amount of a specific currency from a specific demand account held in the maker/depositor's name with that institution. Both the maker and payee may be natural persons or legal entities.
    a. Thing
    b. Check0
    c. Undefined
    d. Undefined

76. In mathematics, the _____ of two sets A and B is the set that contains all elements of A that also belong to B (or equivalently, all elements of B that also belong to A), but no other elements.

Chapter 6. Exponential and Logarirhmic Functions

    a. Thing
    b. Intersection0
    c. Undefined
    d. Undefined

77. _____, Greek for "knowledge of nature," is the branch of science concerned with the discovery and characterization of universal laws which govern matter, energy, space, and time.
    a. Physics0
    b. Thing
    c. Undefined
    d. Undefined

78. In plane geometry, a _____ is a polygon with four equal sides, four right angles, and parallel opposite sides. In algebra, the _____ of a number is that number multiplied by itself.
    a. Square0
    b. Thing
    c. Undefined
    d. Undefined

79. In mathematics, an _____, mean, or central tendency of a data set refers to a measure of the "middle" or "expected" value of the data set.
    a. Average0
    b. Concept
    c. Undefined
    d. Undefined

80. In geometry, an _____ of a triangle is a straight line through a vertex and perpendicular to (i.e. forming a right angle with) the opposite side or an extension of the opposite side.
    a. Concept
    b. Altitude0
    c. Undefined
    d. Undefined

81. _____ is often used to describe the measurement of the steepness, incline, gradient, or grade of a straight line. The _____ is defined as the ratio of the "rise" divided by the "run" between two points on a line, or in other words, the ratio of the altitude change to the horizontal distance between any two points on the line.
    a. Thing
    b. Slope0
    c. Undefined
    d. Undefined

82. In common philosophical language, a proposition or _____, is the content of an assertion, that is, it is true-or-false and defined by the meaning of a particular piece of language.
    a. Concept
    b. Statement0
    c. Undefined
    d. Undefined

83. A _____ is an equation in which each term is either a constant or the product of a constant times the first power of a variable.
    a. Thing
    b. Linear equation0
    c. Undefined
    d. Undefined

84. John _____ of Merchistoun , nicknamed Marvellous Merchistoun, was a Scottish mathematician, physicist, astronomer/astrologer and 8th Laird of Merchistoun. He is most remembered as the inventor of logarithms and _____'s bones, and for popularizing the use of the decimal point.
    a. Napier0
    b. Person
    c. Undefined
    d. Undefined

Chapter 6. Exponential and Logarirhmic Functions

85. _____ of Nerchistoun, nicknamed Marvellous Merchistoun, was a Scottish mathematician, physicist, astronomer/astrologer and 8th Laird of Merchistoun.
   a. John Napier0
   b. Person
   c. Undefined
   d. Undefined

86. A _____ is a deliberate process for transforming one or more inputs into one or more results.
   a. Thing
   b. Calculation0
   c. Undefined
   d. Undefined

87. Compass and straightedge or ruler-and-compass _____ is the _____ of lengths or angles using only an idealized ruler and compass.
   a. Construction0
   b. Thing
   c. Undefined
   d. Undefined

88. In mathematics, a _____ is the end result of a division problem. It can also be expressed as the number of times the divisor divides into the dividend.
   a. Quotient0
   b. Thing
   c. Undefined
   d. Undefined

89. _____ has many meanings, most of which simply .
   a. Thing
   b. Power0
   c. Undefined
   d. Undefined

90. In mathematics, a _____ is a mathematical statement which appears likely to be true, but has not been formally proven to be true under the rules of mathematical logic.
   a. Conjecture0
   b. Concept
   c. Undefined
   d. Undefined

91. An _____ is a function which does the reverse of a given function.
   a. Thing
   b. Inverse function0
   c. Undefined
   d. Undefined

92. A _____ is the result of the addition of a set of numbers. The numbers may be natural numbers, complex numbers, matrices, or still more complicated objects. An infinite _____ is a subtle procedure known as a series.
   a. Sum0
   b. Thing
   c. Undefined
   d. Undefined

93. In mathematics, a _____ is a condition that a solution to an optimization problem must satisfy in order to be acceptable.
   a. Constraint0
   b. Thing
   c. Undefined
   d. Undefined

94. In linear algebra, the _____ of a matrix is obtained by combining two matrices in such a way that a matrix of coefficients to which has been added a column of constants corresponds to the right hand side of the equations.

Chapter 6. Exponential and Logarirhmic Functions

    a. Augmented matrix0
    b. Thing
    c. Undefined
    d. Undefined

95. In mathematics, an _____ number is any real number that is not a rational number- that is, it is a number which cannot be expressed as a fraction m/n, where m and n are integers.
    a. Thing
    b. Irrational0
    c. Undefined
    d. Undefined

96. In mathematics, an _____ is any real number that is not a rational number ¡ª that is, it is a number which cannot be expressed as m/n, where m and n are integers.
    a. Irrational number0
    b. Thing
    c. Undefined
    d. Undefined

97. A frame of _____ is a particular perspective from which the universe is observed.
    a. Thing
    b. Reference0
    c. Undefined
    d. Undefined

98. A _____ is a quantity that denotes the proportional amount or magnitude of one quantity relative to another.
    a. Thing
    b. Ratio0
    c. Undefined
    d. Undefined

99. The metre (or _____, see spelling differences) is a measure of length. It is the basic unit of length in the metric system and in the International System of Units (SI), used around the world for general and scientific purposes.
    a. Meter0
    b. Concept
    c. Undefined
    d. Undefined

100. The decimal separator is a symbol used to mark the boundary between the integral and the fractional parts of a decimal numeral. Terms implying the symbol used are _____ and decimal comma.
    a. Concept
    b. Decimal point0
    c. Undefined
    d. Undefined

101. In mathematics, a _____ is an ordered list of objects. Like a set, it contains members, also called elements or terms, and the number of terms is called the length of the _____. Unlike a set, order matters, and the exact same elements can appear multiple times at different positions in the _____.
    a. Sequence0
    b. Thing
    c. Undefined
    d. Undefined

102. In mathematics, a matrix can be thought of as each row or _____ being a vector. Hence, a space formed by row vectors or _____ vectors are said to be a row space or a _____ space.
    a. Column0
    b. Concept
    c. Undefined
    d. Undefined

103. An _____ of a product of sums expresses it as a sum of products by using the fact that multiplication distributes over addition.

Chapter 6. Exponential and Logarirhmic Functions

a. Thing
c. Undefined
b. Expansion0
d. Undefined

104. A _____ decimal is a number whose decimal representation eventually becomes periodic (i.e. the same number sequence _____ indefinitely).
   a. Repeating0
   c. Undefined
   b. Thing
   d. Undefined

105. A _____ function is a function for which, intuitively, small changes in the input result in small changes in the output.
   a. Continuous0
   c. Undefined
   b. Event
   d. Undefined

106. _____ is the logarithm to the base e, where e is an irrational constant approximately equal to 2.718281828459.
   a. Thing
   c. Undefined
   b. Natural logarithm0
   d. Undefined

107. In mathematics, defined and _____ are used to explain whether or not expressions have meaningful, sensible, and unambiguous values.
   a. Thing
   c. Undefined
   b. Undefined0
   d. Undefined

108. In trigonometry, the _____ is a function defined as $\tan x = \sin x / \cos x$. The function is so-named because it can be defined as the length of a certain segment of a _____ (in the geometric sense) to the unit circle. In plane geometry, a line is _____ to a curve, at some point, if both line and curve pass through the point with the same direction.
   a. Thing
   c. Undefined
   b. Tangent0
   d. Undefined

109. In mathematics, the concept of a _____ tries to capture the intuitive idea of a geometrical one-dimensional and continuous object. A simple example is the circle.
   a. Thing
   c. Undefined
   b. Curve0
   d. Undefined

110. _____ has two distinct but etymologically-related meanings: one in geometry and one in trigonometry.
   a. Thing
   c. Undefined
   b. Tangent line0
   d. Undefined

111. In Euclidean geometry, a _____ is moving every point a constant distance in a specified direction.
   a. Concept
   c. Undefined
   b. Translation0
   d. Undefined

112. A _____ is a one-dimensional picture in which the integers are shown as specially-marked points evenly spaced on a line.
   a. Number line0
   c. Undefined
   b. Thing
   d. Undefined

Chapter 6. Exponential and Logarirhmic Functions

113. In mathematics, an _____ is a statement about the relative size or order of two objects.
 a. Inequality0
 b. Thing
 c. Undefined
 d. Undefined

114. In a right triangle, the _____ of the triangle are the two sides that are perpendicular to each other, as opposed to the hypotenuse.
 a. Legs0
 b. Thing
 c. Undefined
 d. Undefined

115. In physics, _____ is an influence that may cause an object to accelerate. It may be experienced as a lift, a push, or a pull. The actual acceleration of the body is determined by the vector sum of all forces acting on it, known as net _____ or resultant _____.
 a. Force0
 b. Thing
 c. Undefined
 d. Undefined

116. _____ is the shape of a hanging flexible chain or cable when supported at its ends and acted upon by a uniform gravitational force. The chain is steepest near the points of suspension because this part of the chain has the most weight pulling down on it. Toward the bottom, the slope of the chain decreases because the chain is supporting less weight.
 a. Catenary0
 b. Thing
 c. Undefined
 d. Undefined

117. In mathematics, a _____ is a polynomial equation of the second degree. The general form is $ax^2 + bx + c = 0$.
 a. Thing
 b. Quadratic equation0
 c. Undefined
 d. Undefined

118. The _____ of a mathematical object is its size: a property by which it can be larger or smaller than other objects of the same kind; in technical terms, an ordering of the class of objects to which it belongs.
 a. Thing
 b. Magnitude0
 c. Undefined
 d. Undefined

119. An _____ is the result from the sudden release of stored energy in the Earth's crust that creates seismic waves.
 a. Thing
 b. Earthquake0
 c. Undefined
 d. Undefined

120. Mathematical _____ is used to represent ideas.
 a. Notation0
 b. Thing
 c. Undefined
 d. Undefined

121. _____ is a notation for writing numbers that is often used by scientists and mathematicians to make it easier to write large and small numbers.
 a. Scientific notation0
 b. Thing
 c. Undefined
 d. Undefined

122. A _____ is a number that is less than zero.

Chapter 6. Exponential and Logarirhmic Functions

    a. Negative number0
    b. Thing
    c. Undefined
    d. Undefined

123. _____ is a branch of mathematics concerning the study of structure, relation and quantity.
    a. Concept
    b. Algebra0
    c. Undefined
    d. Undefined

124. A _____ is a set of numbers that designate location in a given reference system, such as x,y in a planar _____ system or an x,y,z in a three-dimensional _____ system.
    a. Thing
    b. Coordinate0
    c. Undefined
    d. Undefined

125. A _____ is a unit of length, usually used to measure distance, in a number of different systems, including Imperial units, United States customary units and Norwegian/Swedish mil. Its size can vary from system to system, but in each is between 1 and 10 kilometers. In contemporary English contexts _____ refers to either:
    a. Mile0
    b. Thing
    c. Undefined
    d. Undefined

126. Acid _____ ratio measures the ability of a company to use its near cash or quick assets to immediately extinguish its current liabilities.
    a. Test0
    b. Thing
    c. Undefined
    d. Undefined

127. A _____ is an abstract model that uses mathematical language to describe the behavior of a system. Eykhoff defined a _____ as 'a representation of the essential aspects of an existing system which presents knowledge of that system in usable form'.
    a. Thing
    b. Mathematical model0
    c. Undefined
    d. Undefined

128. _____ are external two-dimensional outlines, with the appearance or configuration of some thing - in contrast to the matter or content or substance of which it is composed.
    a. Thing
    b. Shapes0
    c. Undefined
    d. Undefined

129. In mathematics, the additive inverse, or _____ of a number n is the number that, when added to n, yields zero. The additive inverse of n is denoted −n. For example, 7 is −7, because 7 + (−7) = 0, and the additive inverse of −0.3 is 0.3, because −0.3 + 0.3 = 0.
    a. Thing
    b. Opposite0
    c. Undefined
    d. Undefined

130. In mathematics, the _____ of a number n is the number that, when added to n, yields zero. The _____ of n is denoted −n. For example, 7 is −7, because 7 + (−7) = 0, and the _____ of −0.3 is 0.3, because −0.3 + 0.3 = 0.
    a. Thing
    b. Additive inverse0
    c. Undefined
    d. Undefined

131. The _____ is the total number of human beings alive on the planet Earth at a given time.

Chapter 6. Exponential and Logarirhmic Functions

a. Thing
c. Undefined
b. World population0
d. Undefined

132. In mathematics, a _____ or rhodonea curve is a sinusoid plotted in polar coordinates.
a. Thing
c. Undefined
b. Rose0
d. Undefined

133. _____ is the process of reducing the number of significant digits in a number.
a. Concept
c. Undefined
b. Rounding0
d. Undefined

134. _____, in economics and political economy, are the distributions or payments awarded to the various suppliers of the factors of production.
a. Returns0
c. Undefined
b. Thing
d. Undefined

135. In the scientific method, an _____ (Latin: ex-+-periri, "of (or from) trying"), is a set of actions and observations, performed in the context of solving a particular problem or question, in order to support or falsify a hypothesis or research concerning phenomena.
a. Thing
c. Undefined
b. Experiment0
d. Undefined

136. An _____ is a collection of two not necessarily distinct objects, one of which is distinguished as the first coordinate and the other as the second coordinate.
a. Ordered pair0
c. Undefined
b. Thing
d. Undefined

137. In mathematics, the conjugate _____ or adjoint matrix of an m-by-n matrix A with complex entries is the n-by-m matrix A* obtained from A by taking the transpose and then taking the complex conjugate of each entry.
a. Pairs0
c. Undefined
b. Thing
d. Undefined

138. In mathematics, a _____ function in the sense of algebraic geometry is an everywhere-defined, polynomial function on an algebraic variety V with values in the field K over which V is defined.
a. Thing
c. Undefined
b. Regular0
d. Undefined

139. In algebra, a _____ is a function depending on n that associates a scalar, det(A), to every $n \times n$ square matrix A.
a. Determinant0
c. Undefined
b. Thing
d. Undefined

140. _____, from Latin meaning "to make progress", is defined in two different ways. Pure economic _____ is the increase in wealth that an investor has from making an investment, taking into consideration all costs associated with that investment including the opportunity cost of capital.

a. Profit0
b. Thing
c. Undefined
d. Undefined

Chapter 7. Polynomial functions

1. The _____ of a solid object is the three-dimensional concept of how much space it occupies, often quantified numerically.
   a. Thing
   b. Volume0
   c. Undefined
   d. Undefined

2. _____ is the income from capital investment paid in a series of regular payments.
   a. Annuity0
   b. Thing
   c. Undefined
   d. Undefined

3. In mathematics, a _____ is an expression that is constructed from one or more variables and constants, using only the operations of addition, subtraction, multiplication, and constant positive whole number exponents. is a _____. Note in particular that division by an expression containing a variable is not in general allowed in polynomials. [1]
   a. Polynomial0
   b. Thing
   c. Undefined
   d. Undefined

4. The mathematical concept of a _____ expresses the intuitive idea of deterministic dependence between two quantities, one of which is viewed as primary and the other as secondary. A _____ then is a way to associate a unique output for each input of a specified type, for example, a real number or an element of a given set.
   a. Function0
   b. Thing
   c. Undefined
   d. Undefined

5. _____ is a synonym for information.
   a. Data0
   b. Thing
   c. Undefined
   d. Undefined

6. _____ are external two-dimensional outlines, with the appearance or configuration of some thing - in contrast to the matter or content or substance of which it is composed.
   a. Shapes0
   b. Thing
   c. Undefined
   d. Undefined

7. _____ are the basic objects of study in graph theory. Informally speaking, a graph is a set of objects called points, nodes, or vertices connected by links called lines or edges.
   a. Graphs0
   b. Thing
   c. Undefined
   d. Undefined

8. _____ is a kind of property which exists as magnitude or multitude. It is among the basic classes of things along with quality, substance, change, and relation.
   a. Amount0
   b. Thing
   c. Undefined
   d. Undefined

9. _____ is the fee paid on borrowed money.
   a. Interest0
   b. Thing
   c. Undefined
   d. Undefined

10. _____ or investing is a term with several closely-related meanings in business management, finance and economics, related to saving or deferring consumption.

Chapter 7. Polynomial functions

    a. Thing
    b. Investment0
    c. Undefined
    d. Undefined

11. A _____ is the result of the addition of a set of numbers. The numbers may be natural numbers, complex numbers, matrices, or still more complicated objects. An infinite _____ is a subtle procedure known as a series.
    a. Thing
    b. Sum0
    c. Undefined
    d. Undefined

12. A _____ is a special kind of ratio, indicating a relationship between two measurements with different units, such as miles to gallons or cents to pounds.
    a. Thing
    b. Rate0
    c. Undefined
    d. Undefined

13. An _____ is a combination of numbers, operators, grouping symbols and/or free variables and bound variables arranged in a meaningful way which can be evaluated..
    a. Thing
    b. Expression0
    c. Undefined
    d. Undefined

14. An _____ is the fee paid on borrow money.
    a. Interest rate0
    b. Concept
    c. Undefined
    d. Undefined

15. In mathematics, a _____ is a particular kind of polynomial, having just one term.
    a. Thing
    b. Monomial0
    c. Undefined
    d. Undefined

16. A _____ is a symbolic representation denoting a quantity or expression. It often represents an "unknown" quantity that has the potential to change.
    a. Thing
    b. Variable0
    c. Undefined
    d. Undefined

17. In mathematics and the mathematical sciences, a _____ is a fixed, but possibly unspecified, value. This is in contrast to a variable, which is not fixed.
    a. Constant0
    b. Thing
    c. Undefined
    d. Undefined

18. In mathematics, a _____ is a constant multiplicative factor of a certain object. The object can be such things as a variable, a vector, a function, etc. For example, the _____ of $9x^2$ is 9.
    a. Coefficient0
    b. Thing
    c. Undefined
    d. Undefined

19. In mathematics, there are several meanings of _____ depending on the subject.
    a. Degree0
    b. Thing
    c. Undefined
    d. Undefined

20. The _____ is the maximum of the degrees of all terms in the polynomial.

a. Degree of a polynomial0
b. Thing
c. Undefined
d. Undefined

21. A _____ is a polynomial consisting of three terms; in other words, it is the sum of three monomials.
   a. Trinomial0
   b. Thing
   c. Undefined
   d. Undefined

22. In elementary algebra, a _____ is a polynomial with two terms: the sum of two monomials. It is the simplest kind of polynomial except for a monomial.
   a. Binomial0
   b. Thing
   c. Undefined
   d. Undefined

23. A _____ is a deliberate process for transforming one or more inputs into one or more results.
   a. Thing
   b. Calculation0
   c. Undefined
   d. Undefined

24. _____ is a notation for writing numbers that is often used by scientists and mathematicians to make it easier to write large and small numbers.
   a. Scientific notation0
   b. Thing
   c. Undefined
   d. Undefined

25. _____ is a mathematical operation, written a^n, involving two numbers, the base a and the exponent n.
   a. Thing
   b. Exponentiating0
   c. Undefined
   d. Undefined

26. _____ is a mathematical operation, written a^n, involving two numbers, the base a and the exponent n.
   a. Thing
   b. Exponentiation0
   c. Undefined
   d. Undefined

27. The _____ of a ring R is defined to be the smallest positive integer n such that n a = 0, for all a in R.
   a. Thing
   b. Characteristic0
   c. Undefined
   d. Undefined

28. In mathematics, a _____ is a mathematical statement which appears likely to be true, but has not been formally proven to be true under the rules of mathematical logic.
   a. Conjecture0
   b. Concept
   c. Undefined
   d. Undefined

29. In mathematics, an inequality is a statement about the relative size or order of two objects. For example 14 > 10, or 14 is _____ 10.
   a. Greater than0
   b. Thing
   c. Undefined
   d. Undefined

30. In mathematics, a _____ is the result of multiplying, or an expression that identifies factors to be multiplied.

a. Product0
b. Thing
c. Undefined
d. Undefined

31. _____ is the application of tools and a processing medium to the transformation of raw materials into finished goods for sale.
    a. Manufacturing0
    b. Thing
    c. Undefined
    d. Undefined

32. The _____ of measurement are a globally standardized and modernized form of the metric system.
    a. Units0
    b. Thing
    c. Undefined
    d. Undefined

33. A quadratic equation with real solutions, called roots, which may be real or complex, is given by the _____: $x = \frac{-b \pm \sqrt{b^2 - 4ac}}{2a}$.
    a. Thing
    b. Quadratic formula0
    c. Undefined
    d. Undefined

34. In mathematics, the concept of a _____ tries to capture the intuitive idea of a geometrical one-dimensional and continuous object. A simple example is the circle.
    a. Curve0
    b. Thing
    c. Undefined
    d. Undefined

35. In mathematics, _____ geometry was the traditional name for the geometry of three-dimensional Euclidean space — for practical purposes the kind of space we live in.
    a. Thing
    b. Solid0
    c. Undefined
    d. Undefined

36. A _____ is a function that assigns a number to subsets of a given set.
    a. Thing
    b. Measure0
    c. Undefined
    d. Undefined

37. In geometry, a _____ (Greek words diairo = divide and metro = measure) of a circle is any straight line segment that passes through the centre and whose endpoints are on the circular boundary, or, in more modern usage, the length of such a line segment. When using the word in the more modern sense, one speaks of the _____ rather than a _____, because all diameters of a circle have the same length. This length is twice the radius. The _____ of a circle is also the longest chord that the circle has.
    a. Diameter0
    b. Thing
    c. Undefined
    d. Undefined

38. In classical geometry, a _____ of a circle or sphere is any line segment from its center to its boundary. By extension, the _____ of a circle or sphere is the length of any such segment. The _____ is half the diameter. In science and engineering the term _____ of curvature is commonly used as a synonym for _____.
    a. Radius0
    b. Thing
    c. Undefined
    d. Undefined

39. A _____ is 360° or 2δ radians.

Chapter 7. Polynomial functions

   a. Turn0
   b. Thing
   c. Undefined
   d. Undefined

40. _____ is a set, with some particular properties and usually some additional structure, such as the operations of addition or multiplication, for instance.
   a. Thing
   b. Space0
   c. Undefined
   d. Undefined

41. In geographic information systems, a _____ comprises an entity with a geographic location, typically determined by points, arcs, or polygons. Carriageways and cadastres exemplify _____ data.
   a. Thing
   b. Feature0
   c. Undefined
   d. Undefined

42. In elementary algebra, an _____ is a set that contains every real number between two indicated numbers and may contain the two numbers themselves.
   a. Thing
   b. Interval0
   c. Undefined
   d. Undefined

43. _____ is a free computer algebra system based on a 1982 version of Macsyma
   a. Maxima0
   b. Thing
   c. Undefined
   d. Undefined

44. In mathematics, maxima and _____, known collectively as extrema, are points in the domain of a function at which the function takes a largest value.
   a. Thing
   b. Minima0
   c. Undefined
   d. Undefined

45. In mathematics and elsewhere, the adjective _____ means fourth order, such as the function x4. A _____ number is a number which equals the fourth power of an integer.
   a. Thing
   b. Quartic0
   c. Undefined
   d. Undefined

46. A _____ is a polynomial function with a degree of four. It has the same limit when the argument goes to positive or negative infinity.
   a. Quartic function0
   b. Thing
   c. Undefined
   d. Undefined

47. _____ is a function of the form
   a. Thing
   b. Cubic function0
   c. Undefined
   d. Undefined

48. A real-valued function f defined on the real line is said to have a _____ point at the point x∗, if there exists some ε > 0, such that f when x − x∗ < ε.
   a. Thing
   b. Local maximum0
   c. Undefined
   d. Undefined

Chapter 7. Polynomial functions

49. A _____ is a negotiable instrument instructing a financial institution to pay a specific amount of a specific currency from a specific demand account held in the maker/depositor's name with that institution. Both the maker and payee may be natural persons or legal entities.
   a. Check0
   b. Thing
   c. Undefined
   d. Undefined

50. In mathematics, a _____ may be described informally as a number that can be given by an infinite decimal representation.
   a. Real number0
   b. Thing
   c. Undefined
   d. Undefined

51. In mathematics, a _____ of a k-place relation $L \subseteq X_1 \times \ldots \times X_k$ is one of the sets X_j, $1 \le j \le k$. In the special case where k = 2 and $L \subseteq X_1 \times X_2$ is a function $L : X_1 \to X_2$, it is conventional to refer to X_1 as the _____ of the function and to refer to X_2 as the codomain of the function.
   a. Thing
   b. Domain0
   c. Undefined
   d. Undefined

52. A _____, scatter diagram or scatter graph is a chart that uses Cartesian coordinates to display values for two variables.
   a. Thing
   b. Scatter plot0
   c. Undefined
   d. Undefined

53. The act of _____ is the calculated approximation of a result which is usable even if input data may be incomplete, uncertain, or noisy.
   a. Thing
   b. Estimating0
   c. Undefined
   d. Undefined

54. In business, particularly accounting, a _____ is the time intervals that the accounts, statement, payments, or other calculations cover.
   a. Period0
   b. Thing
   c. Undefined
   d. Undefined

55. _____ is a mathematical science pertaining to the collection, analysis, interpretation or explanation, and presentation of data. It is applicable to a wide variety of academic disciplines, from the physical and social sciences to the humanities.
   a. Thing
   b. Statistics0
   c. Undefined
   d. Undefined

56. In mathematics, a _____ is a rectangular table of numbers or, more generally, a table consisting of abstract quantities that can be added and multiplied.
   a. Thing
   b. Matrix0
   c. Undefined
   d. Undefined

57. _____ element of an element x with respect to a binary operation * with identity element e is an element y such that x * y = y * x = e. In particular,

Chapter 7. Polynomial functions

    a. Thing
    b. Inverse0
    c. Undefined
    d. Undefined

58. In mathematics, a _____ is a polynomial equation of the second degree. The general form is $ax^2 + bx + c = 0$.
    a. Quadratic equation0
    b. Thing
    c. Undefined
    d. Undefined

59. In mathematics, factorization (British English: factorisation) or factoring is the decomposition of an object (for example, a number, a polynomial, or a matrix) into a product of other objects, or _____, which when multiplied together give the original.
    a. Factors0
    b. Thing
    c. Undefined
    d. Undefined

60. In arithmetic, _____ is a procedure for calculating the division of one integer, called the dividend, by another integer called the divisor, to produce a result called the quotient.
    a. Long division0
    b. Thing
    c. Undefined
    d. Undefined

61. In mathematics, _____ allows the rapid division of any polynomial by a binomial of the form x − r. It was described by Paolo Ruffini in 1809. _____ is a special case of long division when the divisor is a linear factor.
    a. Thing
    b. Ruffini's rule0
    c. Undefined
    d. Undefined

62. The _____ is a theorem for finding out the factors of a polynomial.
    a. Thing
    b. Factor theorem0
    c. Undefined
    d. Undefined

63. A _____ is the part of the dividend that is left over when the dividend is not evenly divisible by the divisor.
    a. Thing
    b. Remainder0
    c. Undefined
    d. Undefined

64. In mathematics, a _____ is a statement that can be proved on the basis of explicitly stated or previously agreed assumptions.
    a. Thing
    b. Theorem0
    c. Undefined
    d. Undefined

65. In plane geometry, a _____ is a polygon with four equal sides, four right angles, and parallel opposite sides. In algebra, the _____ of a number is that number multiplied by itself.
    a. Thing
    b. Square0
    c. Undefined
    d. Undefined

66. Equivalence is the condition of being _____ or essentially equal.
    a. Thing
    b. Equivalent0
    c. Undefined
    d. Undefined

Chapter 7. Polynomial functions

67. In mathematics, the conjugate _____ or adjoint matrix of an m-by-n matrix A with complex entries is the n-by-m matrix A* obtained from A by taking the transpose and then taking the complex conjugate of each entry.
   a. Thing
   b. Pairs0
   c. Undefined
   d. Undefined

68. A _____ is a three-dimensional solid object bounded by six square faces, facets, or sides, with three meeting at each vertex.
   a. Cube0
   b. Thing
   c. Undefined
   d. Undefined

69. _____ are of a number n in its third power-the result of multiplying it by itself three times.
   a. Thing
   b. Cubes0
   c. Undefined
   d. Undefined

70. In mathematics, _____ is the decomposition of an object into a product of other objects, or factors, which when multiplied together give the original.
   a. Factoring0
   b. Thing
   c. Undefined
   d. Undefined

71. The word _____ comes from the Latin word linearis, which means created by lines.
   a. Thing
   b. Linear0
   c. Undefined
   d. Undefined

72. The _____ are the only integral domain whose positive elements are well-ordered, and in which order is preserved by addition. Like the natural numbers, the _____ form a countably infinite set. The set of all _____ is usually denoted in mathematics by a boldface Z .
   a. Thing
   b. Integers0
   c. Undefined
   d. Undefined

73. Acid _____ ratio measures the ability of a company to use its near cash or quick assets to immediately extinguish its current liabilities.
   a. Thing
   b. Test0
   c. Undefined
   d. Undefined

74. In mathematics, a _____ of an integer n, also called a factor of n, is an integer which evenly divides n without leaving a remainder.
   a. Thing
   b. Divisor0
   c. Undefined
   d. Undefined

75. In mathematics, a _____ is the end result of a division problem. It can also be expressed as the number of times the divisor divides into the dividend.
   a. Quotient0
   b. Thing
   c. Undefined
   d. Undefined

76. _____ systems represent systems whose behavior is not expressible as a sum of the behaviors of its descriptors.

Chapter 7. Polynomial functions

a. Nonlinear0   b. Thing
c. Undefined   d. Undefined

77. _____ is a payment made by a company to its shareholders
   a. Dividend0   b. Thing
   c. Undefined   d. Undefined

78. A _____ is a numeral used to indicate a count. The most common use of the word today is to name the part of a fraction that tells the number or count of equal parts.
   a. Numerator0   b. Thing
   c. Undefined   d. Undefined

79. A _____ is the part of a fraction that tells how many equal parts make up a whole, and which is used in the name of the fraction: "halves", "thirds", "fourths" or "quarters", "fifths" and so on.
   a. Concept   b. Denominator0
   c. Undefined   d. Undefined

80. _____ in algebra is an application of polynomial long division.
   a. Remainder theorem0   b. Thing
   c. Undefined   d. Undefined

81. In mathematics, a _____ is a quadric surface, with the following equation in Cartesian coordinates: $(x/_a)^2 + (y/_b)^2 = 1$.
   a. Thing   b. Cylinder0
   c. Undefined   d. Undefined

82. The _____ of a member of a multiset is how many memberships in the multiset it has.
   a. Multiplicity0   b. Thing
   c. Undefined   d. Undefined

83. In mathematics, a _____ of a complex-valued function f is a member x of the domain of f such that f(x) vanishes at x, that is, x : f (x) = 0.
   a. Root0   b. Thing
   c. Undefined   d. Undefined

84. A _____ signifies a point or points of probability on a subject e.g., the _____ of creativity, which allows for the formation of rule or norm or law by interpretation of the phenomena events that can be created.
   a. Principle0   b. Thing
   c. Undefined   d. Undefined

85. In mathematics, _____ are the intuitive idea of a geometrical one-dimensional and continuous object.
   a. Thing   b. Curves0
   c. Undefined   d. Undefined

86. In mathematics, the _____ of two sets A and B is the set that contains all elements of A that also belong to B (or equivalently, all elements of B that also belong to A), but no other elements.

Chapter 7. Polynomial functions

a. Thing
b. Intersection0
c. Undefined
d. Undefined

87. The easiest _____ prime numbers resides in the use of the Sieve of Eratosthenes, an algorithm that discovers all prime numbers to a specified integer.
   a. Method for finding0
   b. Thing
   c. Undefined
   d. Undefined

88. In mathematics, a _____ is a number in the form of a + bi where a and b are real numbers, and i is the imaginary unit, with the property i 2 = −1. The real number a is called the real part of the _____, and the real number b is the imaginary part.
   a. Complex number0
   b. Thing
   c. Undefined
   d. Undefined

89. In algebra, a _____ is a binomial formed by taking the opposite of the second term of a binomial.
   a. Thing
   b. Conjugate0
   c. Undefined
   d. Undefined

90. In mathematics, a _____ is a two-dimensional manifold or surface that is perfectly flat.
   a. Thing
   b. Plane0
   c. Undefined
   d. Undefined

91. A _____ ratio, also called, Lift-to-drag ratio, _____ number, or finesse, is an aviation term that refers to the distance an aircraft will move forward for any given amount of lost altitude .
   a. Glide0
   b. Thing
   c. Undefined
   d. Undefined

92. Initial objects are also called _____, and terminal objects are also called final.
   a. Coterminal0
   b. Thing
   c. Undefined
   d. Undefined

93. A _____ is a unit of length, usually used to measure distance, in a number of different systems, including Imperial units, United States customary units and Norwegian/Swedish mil. Its size can vary from system to system, but in each is between 1 and 10 kilometers. In contemporary English contexts _____ refers to either:
   a. Thing
   b. Mile0
   c. Undefined
   d. Undefined

94. _____ is a unit of speed, expressing the number of international miles covered per hour.
   a. Miles per hour0
   b. Thing
   c. Undefined
   d. Undefined

95. In mathematics, the word _____ is used informally to refer to certain distinct bodies of knowledge about mathematics.
   a. Thing
   b. Theoretical0
   c. Undefined
   d. Undefined

Chapter 7. Polynomial functions

96. _____ is the force that opposes the relative motion or tendency toward such motion of two surfaces in contact.
    a. Friction0
    b. Thing
    c. Undefined
    d. Undefined

97. In number theory, the _____ of arithmetic (or unique factorization theorem) states that every natural number greater than 1 can be written as a unique product of prime numbers.
    a. Fundamental theorem0
    b. Concept
    c. Undefined
    d. Undefined

98. In mathematics, a _____ number is a number which can be expressed as a ratio of two integers. Non-integer _____ numbers (commonly called fractions) are usually written as the vulgar fraction a / b, where b is not zero.
    a. Rational0
    b. Thing
    c. Undefined
    d. Undefined

99. The _____ states a constraint on solutions ,or roots, to the polynomial equation $a_n x^n + a_{n-1} x^{n-1} + ... + a_1 x + a_0 = 0$ with integer coefficients.
    a. Rational root theorem0
    b. Event
    c. Undefined
    d. Undefined

100. _____ is a fixed, but possibly unspecified, value. This is in contrast to a variable, which is not fixed.
    a. Thing
    b. Constant term0
    c. Undefined
    d. Undefined

101. In mathematics, a _____ is a number which can be expressed as a ratio of two integers. Non-integer rational numbers (commonly called fractions) are usually written as the vulgar fraction a / b, where b is not zero.
    a. Rational Number0
    b. Concept
    c. Undefined
    d. Undefined

102. _____ forms part of thinking. Considered the most complex of all intellectual functions, _____ has been defined as higher-order cognitive process that requires the modulation and control of more routine or fundamental skills.
    a. Problem solving0
    b. Thing
    c. Undefined
    d. Undefined

103. _____ is a branch of mathematics concerning the study of structure, relation and quantity.
    a. Concept
    b. Algebra0
    c. Undefined
    d. Undefined

104. _____ states that every non-zero single-variable polynomial, with complex coefficients, has exactly as many complex roots as its degree, if repeated roots are counted up to their multiplicity.
    a. Thing
    b. Fundamental theorem of algebra0
    c. Undefined
    d. Undefined

105. A _____ is a mathematical statement which follows easily from a previously proven statement, typically a mathematical theorem.

Chapter 7. Polynomial functions

    a. Corollary0
    b. Thing
    c. Undefined
    d. Undefined

106. _____ is the mathematical action of repeatedly adding or subtracting one, usually to find out how many objects there are or to set aside a desired number of objects.
    a. Thing
    b. Counting0
    c. Undefined
    d. Undefined

107. A _____ is a landform that extends above the surrounding terrain in a limited area. A _____ is generally steeper than a hill, but there is no universally accepted standard definition for the height of a _____ or a hill although a _____ usually has an identifiable summit.
    a. Mountain0
    b. Thing
    c. Undefined
    d. Undefined

108. In geometry, the _____ of an object is a point in some sense in the middle of the object.
    a. Thing
    b. Center0
    c. Undefined
    d. Undefined

109. In Euclidean geometry, a uniform _____ is a linear transformation that enlargers or diminishes objects, and whose _____ factor is the same in all directions. This is also called homothethy.
    a. Thing
    b. Scale0
    c. Undefined
    d. Undefined

110. In geometry, an _____ of a triangle is a straight line through a vertex and perpendicular to (i.e. forming a right angle with) the opposite side or an extension of the opposite side.
    a. Altitude0
    b. Concept
    c. Undefined
    d. Undefined

111. In geometry, a _____ is a special kind of point, usually a corner of a polygon, polyhedron, or higher dimensional polytope. In the geometry of curves a _____ is a point of where the first derivative of curvature is zero. In graph theory, a _____ is the fundamental unit out of which graphs are formed
    a. Thing
    b. Vertex0
    c. Undefined
    d. Undefined

112. A _____ is a set of numbers that designate location in a given reference system, such as x,y in a planar _____ system or an x,y,z in a three-dimensional _____ system.
    a. Thing
    b. Coordinate0
    c. Undefined
    d. Undefined

113. _____ means "constancy", i.e. if something retains a certain feature even after we change a way of looking at it, then it is symmetric.
    a. Symmetry0
    b. Thing
    c. Undefined
    d. Undefined

114. An _____ is a straight line around which a geometric figure can be rotated.

Chapter 7. Polynomial functions

a. Axis0
b. Thing
c. Undefined
d. Undefined

115. _____ of a two-dimensional figure is a line such that, if a perpendicular is constructed, any two points lying on the perpendicular at equal distances from the _____ are identical.
    a. Thing
    b. Axis of symmetry0
    c. Undefined
    d. Undefined

116. An _____ is a collection of two not necessarily distinct objects, one of which is distinguished as the first coordinate and the other as the second coordinate.
    a. Thing
    b. Ordered pair0
    c. Undefined
    d. Undefined

117. _____ is the estimation of a physical quantity such as distance, energy, temperature, or time.
    a. Measurement0
    b. Thing
    c. Undefined
    d. Undefined

118. A _____ is an instrument used in geometry technical drawing and engineering/building to measure distances and/or to rule straight lines.
    a. Thing
    b. Ruler0
    c. Undefined
    d. Undefined

119. In mathematics, a _____ can mean either an element of the set {1, 2, 3, ...} (i.e the positive integers) or an element of the set {0, 1, 2, 3, ...} (i.e. the non-negative integers).
    a. Whole number0
    b. Concept
    c. Undefined
    d. Undefined

120. Regrouping is the act of putting ones into groups of 10. For example, the 1 on the far right of 131 would be denoted _____ if the digit of the number being subtracted is larger than 1, such as 131-99.
    a. By 100
    b. Thing
    c. Undefined
    d. Undefined

121. An _____ is an increase, either of some fixed amount, for example added regularly, or of a variable amount.
    a. Thing
    b. Increment0
    c. Undefined
    d. Undefined

122. A _____ function is a function for which, intuitively, small changes in the input result in small changes in the output.
    a. Event
    b. Continuous0
    c. Undefined
    d. Undefined

123. An n-sided _____ is a polyhedron formed by connecting an n-sided polygonal base and a point, called the apex, by n triangular faces. In other words, it is a conic solid with polygonal base.
    a. Pyramid0
    b. Thing
    c. Undefined
    d. Undefined

Chapter 7. Polynomial functions

124. A _____ is a three-dimensional geometric shape formed by straight lines through a fixed point (vertex) to the points of a fixed curve (directrix)
 a. Cone0
 b. Concept
 c. Undefined
 d. Undefined

125. _____ is often used to describe the measurement of the steepness, incline, gradient, or grade of a straight line. The _____ is defined as the ratio of the "rise" divided by the "run" between two points on a line, or in other words, the ratio of the altitude change to the horizontal distance between any two points on the line.
 a. Slope0
 b. Thing
 c. Undefined
 d. Undefined

126. In mathematics, the _____ is a conic section generated by the intersection of a right circular conical surface and a plane parallel to a generating straight line of that surface. It can also be defined as locus of points in a plane which are equidistant from a given point.
 a. Parabola0
 b. Thing
 c. Undefined
 d. Undefined

127. _____ is a special mathematical relationship between two quantities. Two quantities are called proportional if they vary in such a way that one of the quantities is a constant multiple of the other, or equivalently if they have a constant ratio.
 a. Proportionality0
 b. Thing
 c. Undefined
 d. Undefined

128. _____ is a subset of a population.
 a. Sample0
 b. Thing
 c. Undefined
 d. Undefined

129. In mathematics, a _____ is an ordered list of objects. Like a set, it contains members, also called elements or terms, and the number of terms is called the length of the _____. Unlike a set, order matters, and the exact same elements can appear multiple times at different positions in the _____.
 a. Sequence0
 b. Thing
 c. Undefined
 d. Undefined

130. In linear algebra, the _____ of an n-by-n square matrix A is defined to be the sum of the elements on the main diagonal of A,
 a. Trace0
 b. Thing
 c. Undefined
 d. Undefined

Chapter 8. Rational Functions and Radical Functions

1. _____ is the symbol used to indicate the nth root of a number
   - a. Thing
   - b. Radical0
   - c. Undefined
   - d. Undefined

2. In mathematics, a _____ of a complex-valued function f is a member x of the domain of f such that f(x) vanishes at x, that is, x : f (x) = 0.
   - a. Thing
   - b. Root0
   - c. Undefined
   - d. Undefined

3. The mathematical concept of a _____ expresses the intuitive idea of deterministic dependence between two quantities, one of which is viewed as primary and the other as secondary. A _____ then is a way to associate a unique output for each input of a specified type, for example, a real number or an element of a given set.
   - a. Function0
   - b. Thing
   - c. Undefined
   - d. Undefined

4. In plane geometry, a _____ is a polygon with four equal sides, four right angles, and parallel opposite sides. In algebra, the _____ of a number is that number multiplied by itself.
   - a. Square0
   - b. Thing
   - c. Undefined
   - d. Undefined

5. In mathematics, a _____ number is a number which can be expressed as a ratio of two integers. Non-integer _____ numbers (commonly called fractions) are usually written as the vulgar fraction a / b, where b is not zero.
   - a. Rational0
   - b. Thing
   - c. Undefined
   - d. Undefined

6. In mathematics, a _____ is any function which can be written as the ratio of two polynomial functions.
   - a. Thing
   - b. Rational function0
   - c. Undefined
   - d. Undefined

7. _____, Greek for "knowledge of nature," is the branch of science concerned with the discovery and characterization of universal laws which govern matter, energy, space, and time.
   - a. Thing
   - b. Physics0
   - c. Undefined
   - d. Undefined

8. _____ element of an element x with respect to a binary operation * with identity element e is an element y such that x * y = y * x = e. In particular,
   - a. Inverse0
   - b. Thing
   - c. Undefined
   - d. Undefined

9. In mathematics, _____ expressions is used to reduce the expression into the lowest possible term.
   - a. Thing
   - b. Simplifying0
   - c. Undefined
   - d. Undefined

10. _____ are the basic objects of study in graph theory. Informally speaking, a graph is a set of objects called points, nodes, or vertices connected by links called lines or edges.

a. Graphs0
b. Thing
c. Undefined
d. Undefined

11. An _____ is a combination of numbers, operators, grouping symbols and/or free variables and bound variables arranged in a meaningful way which can be evaluated..
   a. Thing
   b. Expression0
   c. Undefined
   d. Undefined

12. _____ is electromagnetic radiation with a wavelength that is visible to the eye (visible _____) or, in a technical or scientific context, electromagnetic radiation of any wavelength.
   a. Thing
   b. Light0
   c. Undefined
   d. Undefined

13. In mathematics, an _____ is a statement about the relative size or order of two objects.
   a. Thing
   b. Inequality0
   c. Undefined
   d. Undefined

14. The _____, the average in everyday English, which is also called the arithmetic _____ (and is distinguished from the geometric _____ or harmonic _____). The average is also called the sample _____. The expected value of a random variable, which is also called the population _____.
   a. Mean0
   b. Thing
   c. Undefined
   d. Undefined

15. _____ is a kind of property which exists as magnitude or multitude. It is among the basic classes of things along with quality, substance, change, and relation.
   a. Amount0
   b. Thing
   c. Undefined
   d. Undefined

16. _____ was an Italian physicist, mathematician, astronomer, and philosopher who is closely associated with the scientific revolution.
   a. Galileo Galilei0
   b. Person
   c. Undefined
   d. Undefined

17. A _____ is a compensation which workers receive in exchange for their labor.
   a. Wage0
   b. Thing
   c. Undefined
   d. Undefined

18. In mathematics, an _____, mean, or central tendency of a data set refers to a measure of the "middle" or "expected" value of the data set.
   a. Concept
   b. Average0
   c. Undefined
   d. Undefined

19. _____ or arithmetics is the oldest and most elementary branch of mathematics, used by almost everyone, for tasks ranging from simple daily counting to advanced science and business calculations.

Chapter 8. Rational Functions and Radical Functions

a. Arithmetic0
c. Undefined
b. Thing
d. Undefined

20. _____ of a list of numbers is the sum of all the members of the list divided by the number of items in the list.
    a. Arithmetic mean0
    b. Thing
    c. Undefined
    d. Undefined

21. In acoustics and telecommunication, the _____ of a wave is a component frequency of the signal that is an integer multiple of the fundamental frequency.
    a. Harmonic0
    b. Thing
    c. Undefined
    d. Undefined

22. The _____ is one of several kinds of average. It is the number of variables divided by the sum of the reciprocals of the variables.
    a. Harmonic mean0
    b. Thing
    c. Undefined
    d. Undefined

23. The _____ function (weight function) is a mathematical device used when performing a sum, integral, or average in order to give some elements more of a "weight" than others.
    a. Weighted0
    b. Thing
    c. Undefined
    d. Undefined

24. _____ is a synonym for information.
    a. Data0
    b. Thing
    c. Undefined
    d. Undefined

25. A _____ is a symbolic representation denoting a quantity or expression. It often represents an "unknown" quantity that has the potential to change.
    a. Thing
    b. Variable0
    c. Undefined
    d. Undefined

26. In mathematics and the mathematical sciences, a _____ is a fixed, but possibly unspecified, value. This is in contrast to a variable, which is not fixed.
    a. Thing
    b. Constant0
    c. Undefined
    d. Undefined

27. In mathematics, a _____ in elementary terms is any of a variety of different functions from geometry, such as rotations, reflections and translations.
    a. Thing
    b. Transformation0
    c. Undefined
    d. Undefined

28. An _____ is a collection of two not necessarily distinct objects, one of which is distinguished as the first coordinate and the other as the second coordinate.
    a. Ordered pair0
    b. Thing
    c. Undefined
    d. Undefined

Chapter 8. Rational Functions and Radical Functions

29. In mathematics, defined and _____ are used to explain whether or not expressions have meaningful, sensible, and unambiguous values.
    a. Thing
    b. Undefined0
    c. Undefined
    d. Undefined

30. _____ is a relationship among three or more variables in which each pair of variables varies directly or inversely.
    a. Thing
    b. Joint variation0
    c. Undefined
    d. Undefined

31. The _____ of a solid object is the three-dimensional concept of how much space it occupies, often quantified numerically.
    a. Volume0
    b. Thing
    c. Undefined
    d. Undefined

32. In linear algebra and geometry, a rotation (_____) is a type of transformation from one system of coordinates to another system of coordinates such that distance between any two points remains invariant under the transformation.
    a. Rotational0
    b. Thing
    c. Undefined
    d. Undefined

33. A _____ is a unit of length, usually used to measure distance, in a number of different systems, including Imperial units, United States customary units and Norwegian/Swedish mil. Its size can vary from system to system, but in each is between 1 and 10 kilometers. In contemporary English contexts _____ refers to either:
    a. Thing
    b. Mile0
    c. Undefined
    d. Undefined

34. _____ is a unit of speed, expressing the number of international miles covered per hour.
    a. Thing
    b. Miles per hour0
    c. Undefined
    d. Undefined

35. The _____ is the distance around a closed curve. _____ is a kind of perimeter.
    a. Thing
    b. Circumference0
    c. Undefined
    d. Undefined

36. A _____ is a statement or claimt that a particular event will occur in the future in more certain terms than a forecast.
    a. Thing
    b. Prediction0
    c. Undefined
    d. Undefined

37. In mathematics, an inequality is a statement about the relative size or order of two objects. For example 14 > 10, or 14 is _____ 10.
    a. Thing
    b. Greater than0
    c. Undefined
    d. Undefined

38. In mathematics, a _____ is a two-dimensional manifold or surface that is perfectly flat.

Chapter 8. Rational Functions and Radical Functions

    a. Plane0   b. Thing
    c. Undefined   d. Undefined

39.   In physics, _____ is an influence that may cause an object to accelerate. It may be experienced as a lift, a push, or a pull. The actual acceleration of the body is determined by the vector sum of all forces acting on it, known as net _____ or resultant _____.
    a. Thing   b. Force0
    c. Undefined   d. Undefined

40.   _____ is the speed of an aircraft relative to the air.
    a. Thing   b. Airspeed0
    c. Undefined   d. Undefined

41.   _____ is a physical property of a system that underlies the common notions of hot and cold; something that is hotter has the greater _____.
    a. Thing   b. Temperature0
    c. Undefined   d. Undefined

42.   A _____ is a special kind of ratio, indicating a relationship between two measurements with different units, such as miles to gallons or cents to pounds.
    a. Thing   b. Rate0
    c. Undefined   d. Undefined

43.   _____ is a mathematical operation, written a^n, involving two numbers, the base a and the exponent n.
    a. Exponentiating0   b. Thing
    c. Undefined   d. Undefined

44.   _____ is a mathematical operation, written a^n, involving two numbers, the base a and the exponent n.
    a. Exponentiation0   b. Thing
    c. Undefined   d. Undefined

45.   In geometry, a _____ is a special kind of point, usually a corner of a polygon, polyhedron, or higher dimensional polytope. In the geometry of curves a _____ is a point of where the first derivative of curvature is zero. In graph theory, a _____ is the fundamental unit out of which graphs are formed
    a. Thing   b. Vertex0
    c. Undefined   d. Undefined

46.   _____ means "constancy", i.e. if something retains a certain feature even after we change a way of looking at it, then it is symmetric.
    a. Thing   b. Symmetry0
    c. Undefined   d. Undefined

47.   An _____ is a straight line around which a geometric figure can be rotated.
    a. Axis0   b. Thing
    c. Undefined   d. Undefined

Chapter 8. Rational Functions and Radical Functions

48. _____ of a two-dimensional figure is a line such that, if a perpendicular is constructed, any two points lying on the perpendicular at equal distances from the _____ are identical.
   a. Thing
   b. Axis of symmetry0
   c. Undefined
   d. Undefined

49. In mathematics, there are several meanings of _____ depending on the subject.
   a. Thing
   b. Degree0
   c. Undefined
   d. Undefined

50. In mathematics, a _____ is an expression that is constructed from one or more variables and constants, using only the operations of addition, subtraction, multiplication, and constant positive whole number exponents. is a _____. Note in particular that division by an expression containing a variable is not in general allowed in polynomials. [1]
   a. Polynomial0
   b. Thing
   c. Undefined
   d. Undefined

51. In Euclidean geometry, an _____ is a closed segment of a differentiable curve in the two-dimensional plane; for example, a circular _____ is a segment of a circle.
   a. Arc0
   b. Concept
   c. Undefined
   d. Undefined

52. In Euclidean geometry, a _____ is the set of all points in a plane at a fixed distance, called the radius, from a given point, the center.
   a. Thing
   b. Circle0
   c. Undefined
   d. Undefined

53. An _____ is a straight line or curve A to which another curve B approaches closer and closer as one moves along it. As one moves along B, the space between it and the _____ A becomes smaller and smaller, and can in fact be made as small as one could wish by going far enough along. A curve may or may not touch or cross its _____. In fact, the curve may intersect the _____ an infinite number of times.
   a. Thing
   b. Asymptote0
   c. Undefined
   d. Undefined

54. In mathematics, a _____ of a k-place relation $L \subseteq X_1 \times ... \times X_k$ is one of the sets X_j, $1 \leq j \leq k$. In the special case where k = 2 and $L \subseteq X_1 \times X_2$ is a function $L : X_1 \to X_2$, it is conventional to refer to X_1 as the _____ of the function and to refer to X_2 as the codomain of the function.
   a. Thing
   b. Domain0
   c. Undefined
   d. Undefined

55. In mathematics, a _____ is the end result of a division problem. It can also be expressed as the number of times the divisor divides into the dividend.
   a. Quotient0
   b. Thing
   c. Undefined
   d. Undefined

56. In mathematics, a _____ may be described informally as a number that can be given by an infinite decimal representation.

Chapter 8. Rational Functions and Radical Functions

a. Thing
c. Undefined
b. Real number0
d. Undefined

57. A _____ is the part of a fraction that tells how many equal parts make up a whole, and which is used in the name of the fraction: "halves", "thirds", "fourths" or "quarters", "fifths" and so on.
a. Denominator0
c. Undefined
b. Concept
d. Undefined

58. A _____ is a negotiable instrument instructing a financial institution to pay a specific amount of a specific currency from a specific demand account held in the maker/depositor's name with that institution. Both the maker and payee may be natural persons or legal entities.
a. Thing
c. Undefined
b. Check0
d. Undefined

59. _____ is a straight line or curve A to which another curve B the one being studied approaches closer and closer as one moves along it.
a. Vertical asymptote0
c. Undefined
b. Thing
d. Undefined

60. In astronomy, geography, geometry and related sciences and contexts, a plane is said to be _____ at a given point if it is locally perpendicular to the gradient of the gravity field, i.e., with the direction of the gravitational force at that point.
a. Horizontal0
c. Undefined
b. Thing
d. Undefined

61. A _____ is a numeral used to indicate a count. The most common use of the word today is to name the part of a fraction that tells the number or count of equal parts.
a. Thing
c. Undefined
b. Numerator0
d. Undefined

62. _____ means in succession or back-to-back
a. Thing
c. Undefined
b. Consecutive0
d. Undefined

63. In mathematics, a _____ is a constant multiplicative factor of a certain object. The object can be such things as a variable, a vector, a function, etc. For example, the _____ of $9x^2$ is 9.
a. Coefficient0
c. Undefined
b. Thing
d. Undefined

64. In mathematics, the concept of a _____ tries to capture the intuitive idea of a geometrical one-dimensional and continuous object. A simple example is the circle.
a. Thing
c. Undefined
b. Curve0
d. Undefined

65. In mathematics, _____ are the intuitive idea of a geometrical one-dimensional and continuous object.

a. Curves0
b. Thing
c. Undefined
d. Undefined

66. In geometry, a _____ is defined as a quadrilateral where all four of its angles are right angles.
   a. Thing
   b. Rectangle0
   c. Undefined
   d. Undefined

67. A _____ is a quantity that denotes the proportional amount or magnitude of one quantity relative to another.
   a. Thing
   b. Ratio0
   c. Undefined
   d. Undefined

68. Fixed costs are expenses whose total does not change in proportion to the activity of a business.Unit fixed costs decline with volume following a retangular hyperbola as the volume of production.Variable costs by contrast change in relation to the activity of a business such as sales or production volume.Along with variable costs,fixed costs make up one of the two components of total cost. In the most simple production function total cost is equal to fixed costs plus variable costs.In accounting terminology, fixed costs will broadly include all costs which are not included in cost of goods sold, and variable costs are those captured in costs of goods sold. The implicit assumption required to make the equivalence between the accounting and economics terminology is that the accounting period is equal to the period in which fixed costs do not vary in relation to production. In practice, this equivalence does not always hold and depending on the period under consideration by management, some overhead expenses can be adjusted by management, and the specific allocation of each expense to each category will be decided under cost accounting.In business planning and management accounting, usage of the terms fixed costs, variable costs and others will often differ from usage in economics, and may depend on the intended use. For example, costs may be segregated into per unit costs fixed costs per period, and variable costs as a proportion of revenue. Capital expenditures will usually be allocated separately, and depending on the purpose, a portion may be regularly allocated to expenses as depreciation and amortization and seen as a _____ per period, or the entire amount may be considered upfront fixed costs.
   a. Fixed cost0
   b. Thing
   c. Undefined
   d. Undefined

69. _____ are expenses whose total does not change in proportion to the activity of a business, within the relevant time period or scale of production
   a. Fixed costs0
   b. Thing
   c. Undefined
   d. Undefined

70. _____ is a notation for writing numbers that is often used by scientists and mathematicians to make it easier to write large and small numbers.
   a. Thing
   b. Scientific notation0
   c. Undefined
   d. Undefined

71. _____ is the distance around a given two-dimensional object. As a general rule, the _____ of a polygon can always be calculated by adding all the length of the sides together. So, the formula for triangles is P = a + b + c, where a, b and c stand for each side of it. For quadrilaterals the equation is P = a + b + c + d. For equilateral polygons, P = na, where n is the number of sides and a is the side length.
   a. Thing
   b. Perimeter0
   c. Undefined
   d. Undefined

Chapter 8. Rational Functions and Radical Functions

72. _____ is a business term for the amount of money that a company receives from its activities in a given period, mostly from sales of products and/or services to customers
    a. Revenue0
    b. Thing
    c. Undefined
    d. Undefined

73. _____ is the largest positive integer that divides both numbers without remainder.
    a. Common Factor0
    b. Thing
    c. Undefined
    d. Undefined

74. In mathematics, a _____ is a number which can be expressed as a ratio of two integers. Non-integer rational numbers (commonly called fractions) are usually written as the vulgar fraction a / b, where b is not zero.
    a. Rational Number0
    b. Concept
    c. Undefined
    d. Undefined

75. In mathematics, a _____ is the result of multiplying, or an expression that identifies factors to be multiplied.
    a. Thing
    b. Product0
    c. Undefined
    d. Undefined

76. In mathematics, factorization (British English: factorisation) or factoring is the decomposition of an object (for example, a number, a polynomial, or a matrix) into a product of other objects, or _____, which when multiplied together give the original.
    a. Thing
    b. Factors0
    c. Undefined
    d. Undefined

77. In mathematics, the multiplicative inverse of a number x, denoted 1/x or x^{-1}, is the number which, when multiplied by x, yields 1. The multiplicative inverse of x is also called the _____ of x.
    a. Reciprocal0
    b. Thing
    c. Undefined
    d. Undefined

78. In mathematics, a _____ of an integer n, also called a factor of n, is an integer which evenly divides n without leaving a remainder.
    a. Thing
    b. Divisor0
    c. Undefined
    d. Undefined

79. In geometry, _____ angles are angles that have a common ray coming out of the vertex going between two other rays.
    a. Concept
    b. Adjacent0
    c. Undefined
    d. Undefined

80. _____ of an object is its speed in a particular direction.
    a. Velocity0
    b. Thing
    c. Undefined
    d. Undefined

81. _____ is defined as the rate of change or derivative with respect to time of velocity.

a. Acceleration0
b. Thing
c. Undefined
d. Undefined

82. _____ is often used to describe the measurement of the steepness, incline, gradient, or grade of a straight line. The _____ is defined as the ratio of the "rise" divided by the "run" between two points on a line, or in other words, the ratio of the altitude change to the horizontal distance between any two points on the line.
   a. Thing
   b. Slope0
   c. Undefined
   d. Undefined

83. In geometry, two lines or planes if one falls on the other in such a way as to create congruent adjacent angles. The term may be used as a noun or adjective. Thus, referring to Figure 1, the line AB is the _____ to CD through the point B.
   a. Perpendicular0
   b. Thing
   c. Undefined
   d. Undefined

84. A _____ defined function $f(x)$ of a real variable x is a function whose definition is given differently on disjoint subsets of its domain.
   a. Piecewise0
   b. Thing
   c. Undefined
   d. Undefined

85. A _____ of a number is the product of that number with any integer.
   a. Thing
   b. Multiple0
   c. Undefined
   d. Undefined

86. The _____ of two integers is the smallest positive integer that is a multiple of both intergers.
   a. Least common multiple0
   b. Thing
   c. Undefined
   d. Undefined

87. _____ is the transport of people on a trip/journey or the process or time involved in a person or object moving from one location to another.
   a. Thing
   b. Travel0
   c. Undefined
   d. Undefined

88. _____, in economics and political economy, are the distributions or payments awarded to the various suppliers of the factors of production.
   a. Thing
   b. Returns0
   c. Undefined
   d. Undefined

89. Equivalence is the condition of being _____ or essentially equal.
   a. Thing
   b. Equivalent0
   c. Undefined
   d. Undefined

90. A _____ is the result of the addition of a set of numbers. The numbers may be natural numbers, complex numbers, matrices, or still more complicated objects. An infinite _____ is a subtle procedure known as a series.
   a. Thing
   b. Sum0
   c. Undefined
   d. Undefined

Chapter 8. Rational Functions and Radical Functions

91. _____ of a polynomial with real or complex coefficients is a certain expression in the coefficients of the polynomial which is equal to zero if and only if the polynomial has a multiple root i.e. a root with multiplicity greater than one in the complex numbers.
    a. Thing
    b. Discriminant0
    c. Undefined
    d. Undefined

92. In mathematics, a _____ of a number x is the exponent y of the power by such that $x = b^y$. The value used for the base b must be neither 0 nor 1, nor a root of 1 in the case of the extension to complex numbers, and is typically 10, e, or 2.
    a. Logarithm0
    b. Thing
    c. Undefined
    d. Undefined

93. A _____ signifies a point or points of probability on a subject e.g., the _____ of creativity, which allows for the formation of rule or norm or law by interpretation of the phenomena events that can be created.
    a. Thing
    b. Principle0
    c. Undefined
    d. Undefined

94. _____ are activities that are governed by a set of rules or customs and often engaged in competitively.
    a. Sports0
    b. Thing
    c. Undefined
    d. Undefined

95. _____ is a branch of mathematics concerning the study of structure, relation and quantity.
    a. Concept
    b. Algebra0
    c. Undefined
    d. Undefined

96. In mathematics, the _____ of two sets A and B is the set that contains all elements of A that also belong to B (or equivalently, all elements of B that also belong to A), but no other elements.
    a. Thing
    b. Intersection0
    c. Undefined
    d. Undefined

97. _____ variables are variables other than the independent variable that may bear any effect on the behavior of the subject being studied.
    a. Extraneous0
    b. Thing
    c. Undefined
    d. Undefined

98. In physics, an _____ is the path that an object makes around another object while under the influence of a source of centripetal force, such as gravity.
    a. Orbit0
    b. Thing
    c. Undefined
    d. Undefined

99. _____ is the practice of doing mathematical calculations using only the human brain, with no help from any computing devices.
    a. Mental math0
    b. Concept
    c. Undefined
    d. Undefined

100. The _____ or kilogramme is the SI base unit of mass. It is defined as being equal to the mass of the international prototype of the _____.

a. Thing
b. Kilogram0
c. Undefined
d. Undefined

101. A _____ is a unit of length in the metric system, equal to one thousand metres, the current SI base unit of length
a. Thing
b. Kilometer0
c. Undefined
d. Undefined

102. _____ is a set, with some particular properties and usually some additional structure, such as the operations of addition or multiplication, for instance.
a. Thing
b. Space0
c. Undefined
d. Undefined

103. In geometry, an _____ of a triangle is a straight line through a vertex and perpendicular to (i.e. forming a right angle with) the opposite side or an extension of the opposite side.
a. Altitude0
b. Concept
c. Undefined
d. Undefined

104. A _____ is 360° or 2ð radians.
a. Thing
b. Turn0
c. Undefined
d. Undefined

105. A _____ is an object that is attached to a pivot point so that it can swing freely.
a. Thing
b. Pendulum0
c. Undefined
d. Undefined

106. In business, particularly accounting, a _____ is the time intervals that the accounts, statement, payments, or other calculations cover.
a. Thing
b. Period0
c. Undefined
d. Undefined

107. The metre (or _____, see spelling differences) is a measure of length. It is the basic unit of length in the metric system and in the International System of Units (SI), used around the world for general and scientific purposes.
a. Concept
b. Meter0
c. Undefined
d. Undefined

108. A _____ is a number that is less than zero.
a. Negative number0
b. Thing
c. Undefined
d. Undefined

109. The _____ of measurement are a globally standardized and modernized form of the metric system.
a. Thing
b. Units0
c. Undefined
d. Undefined

110. In mathematics, a _____ (also spelled reflexion) is a map that transforms an object into its mirror image.

Chapter 8. Rational Functions and Radical Functions

a. Concept
b. Reflection0
c. Undefined
d. Undefined

111. A _____ is a three-dimensional solid object bounded by six square faces, facets, or sides, with three meeting at each vertex.
a. Thing
b. Cube0
c. Undefined
d. Undefined

112. A _____ of a number is a number a such that $a^3 = x$.
a. Thing
b. Cube root0
c. Undefined
d. Undefined

113. The _____ is the number or expression underneath the radical sign.
a. Radicand0
b. Thing
c. Undefined
d. Undefined

114. The word _____ is used in a variety of ways in mathematics.
a. Thing
b. Index0
c. Undefined
d. Undefined

115. In mathematics, the _____ of a function is the set of all "output" values produced by that function. Given a function $f : A \to B$, the _____ of f, is defined to be the set $\{x \in B : x = f(a)$ for some $a \in A\}$.
a. Range0
b. Thing
c. Undefined
d. Undefined

116. In mathematics, a _____ is a mathematical statement which appears likely to be true, but has not been formally proven to be true under the rules of mathematical logic.
a. Conjecture0
b. Concept
c. Undefined
d. Undefined

117. In mathematics, a _____ of a number x is a number r such that $r^2 = x$, or in words, a number r whose square (the result of multiplying the number by itself) is x.
a. Square root0
b. Thing
c. Undefined
d. Undefined

118. _____ is the property of a physical object that quantifies the amount of matter and energy it is equivalent to.
a. Thing
b. Mass0
c. Undefined
d. Undefined

119. A _____ is a polynomial function of the form $f(x) = ax^2 + bx + c$, where a, b, c are real numbers and a , 0.
a. Event
b. Quadratic function0
c. Undefined
d. Undefined

120. In classical geometry, a _____ of a circle or sphere is any line segment from its center to its boundary. By extension, the _____ of a circle or sphere is the length of any such segment. The _____ is half the diameter. In science and engineering the term _____ of curvature is commonly used as a synonym for _____.

Chapter 8. Rational Functions and Radical Functions

a. Thing
b. Radius0
c. Undefined
d. Undefined

121. In mathematics, a _____ is the set of all points in three-dimensional space (R^3) which are at distance r from a fixed point of that space, where r is a positive real number called the radius of the _____. The fixed point is called the center or centre, and is not part of the _____ itself.
a. Sphere0
b. Thing
c. Undefined
d. Undefined

122. In mathematics, a _____ is a quadric surface, with the following equation in Cartesian coordinates: $(x/_a)^2 + (y/_b)^2 = 1$.
a. Thing
b. Cylinder0
c. Undefined
d. Undefined

123. André-_____ Ampère was a French physicist who is generally credited as one of the main discoverers of electromagnetism.
a. Marie0
b. Person
c. Undefined
d. Undefined

124. A _____ is a set of numbers that designate location in a given reference system, such as x,y in a planar _____ system or an x,y,z in a three-dimensional _____ system.
a. Thing
b. Coordinate0
c. Undefined
d. Undefined

125. _____ is the study of geometry using the principles of algebra. _____ can be explained more simply: it is concerned with defining geometrical shapes in a numerical way and extracting numerical information from that representation.
a. Analytic geometry0
b. Thing
c. Undefined
d. Undefined

126. In mathematics, _____ are used to indicate the square root of a number.
a. Thing
b. Radicals0
c. Undefined
d. Undefined

127. In mathematics, _____ growth occurs when the growth rate of a function is always proportional to the function's current size.
a. Thing
b. Exponential0
c. Undefined
d. Undefined

128. In mathematics, _____ is a property that a binary operation can have. Within an expression containing two or more of the same associative operators in a row, the order of operations does not matter as long as the sequence of the operands is not changed.
a. Associativity0
b. Thing
c. Undefined
d. Undefined

Chapter 8. Rational Functions and Radical Functions

129. The term _____ can refer to an integer which is the square of some other integer, or an algebraic expression that can be factored as the square of some other expression.
- a. Perfect square0
- b. Thing
- c. Undefined
- d. Undefined

130. _____ is the calculated approximation of a result which is usable even if input data may be incomplete, uncertain, or noisy.
- a. Concept
- b. Estimation0
- c. Undefined
- d. Undefined

131. In mathematics, and in particular in abstract algebra, the _____ is a property of binary operations that generalises the distributive law from elementary algebra.
- a. Distributive property0
- b. Thing
- c. Undefined
- d. Undefined

132. _____, or Rationalisation in mathematics is the process of removing a square root or imaginary number from the denominator of a fraction.
- a. Thing
- b. Rationalizing0
- c. Undefined
- d. Undefined

133. In algebra, a _____ is a binomial formed by taking the opposite of the second term of a binomial.
- a. Conjugate0
- b. Thing
- c. Undefined
- d. Undefined

134. The _____ are the only integral domain whose positive elements are well-ordered, and in which order is preserved by addition. Like the natural numbers, the _____ form a countably infinite set. The set of all _____ is usually denoted in mathematics by a boldface Z .
- a. Integers0
- b. Thing
- c. Undefined
- d. Undefined

135. An _____ of a number a is a number b such that $b^n = a$.
- a. Nth root0
- b. Thing
- c. Undefined
- d. Undefined

136. _____ is the force that opposes the relative motion or tendency toward such motion of two surfaces in contact.
- a. Thing
- b. Friction0
- c. Undefined
- d. Undefined

137. _____ also known as the zero-product rule, is an abstract and explicit statement of the familiar property from elementary mathematics that if the product of two real numbers is zero, then at least one of the numbers in the product factors must be zero.
- a. Thing
- b. Zero product property0
- c. Undefined
- d. Undefined

138. In mathematics, _____ is the decomposition of an object into a product of other objects, or factors, which when multiplied together give the original.

Chapter 8. Rational Functions and Radical Functions

    a. Factoring0
    b. Thing
    c. Undefined
    d. Undefined

139. _____ has many meanings, most of which simply .
    a. Power0
    b. Thing
    c. Undefined
    d. Undefined

140. _____ is the design, analysis, and/or construction of works for practical purposes.
    a. Thing
    b. Engineering0
    c. Undefined
    d. Undefined

141. In common philosophical language, a proposition or _____, is the content of an assertion, that is, it is true-or-false and defined by the meaning of a particular piece of language.
    a. Concept
    b. Statement0
    c. Undefined
    d. Undefined

142. A quadratic equation with real solutions, called roots, which may be real or complex, is given by the _____: $x = \frac{-b \pm \sqrt{b^2 - 4ac}}{2a}$.
    a. Thing
    b. Quadratic formula0
    c. Undefined
    d. Undefined

143. _____ is a relation in Euclidean geometry among the three sides of a right triangle.
    a. Thing
    b. Pythagorean Theorem0
    c. Undefined
    d. Undefined

144. In mathematics, a _____ is a statement that can be proved on the basis of explicitly stated or previously agreed assumptions.
    a. Theorem0
    b. Thing
    c. Undefined
    d. Undefined

145. A _____ is a deliberate process for transforming one or more inputs into one or more results.
    a. Calculation0
    b. Thing
    c. Undefined
    d. Undefined

146. A _____ is an individual or household that purchases and uses goods and services generated within the economy.
    a. Thing
    b. Consumer0
    c. Undefined
    d. Undefined

147. _____, or Fuel efficiency can sometimes mean the same as thermal efficiency, that is, the efficiency of converting energy contained in a carrier fuel to kinetic energy or work.
    a. Fuel consumption0
    b. Thing
    c. Undefined
    d. Undefined

Chapter 8. Rational Functions and Radical Functions

148. U.S. liquid _____ is legally defined as 231 cubic inches, and is equal to 3.785411784 litres or abotu 0.13368 cubic feet. This is the most common definition of a _____. The U.S. fluid ounce is defined as 1/128 of a U.S. _____.
   a. Thing
   b. Gallon0
   c. Undefined
   d. Undefined

149. In geometry, the _____ of an object is a point in some sense in the middle of the object.
   a. Center0
   b. Thing
   c. Undefined
   d. Undefined

150. In chemistry, a _____ is substance made by combining two or more different materials in such a way that no chemical reaction occurs.
   a. Thing
   b. Mixture0
   c. Undefined
   d. Undefined

151. _____ is a free computer algebra system based on a 1982 version of Macsyma
   a. Thing
   b. Maxima0
   c. Undefined
   d. Undefined

152. _____ are points in the domain of a function at which the function takes a largest value or smallest value, either within a given neighborhood or on the function domain in its entirety.
   a. Maxima and minima0
   b. Thing
   c. Undefined
   d. Undefined

153. In mathematics, maxima and _____, known collectively as extrema, are points in the domain of a function at which the function takes a largest value .
   a. Thing
   b. Minima0
   c. Undefined
   d. Undefined

154. _____ are of a number n in its third power-the result of multiplying it by itself three times.
   a. Thing
   b. Cubes0
   c. Undefined
   d. Undefined

155. _____ is the state of being greater than any finite real or natural number, however large.
   a. Infinite0
   b. Thing
   c. Undefined
   d. Undefined

156. A _____ is the part of the dividend that is left over when the dividend is not evenly divisible by the divisor.
   a. Thing
   b. Remainder0
   c. Undefined
   d. Undefined

157. The _____ of a member of a multiset is how many memberships in the multiset it has.
   a. Thing
   b. Multiplicity0
   c. Undefined
   d. Undefined

158. _____ statistics are statistics that estimate population parameters.

a. Parametric0
b. Thing
c. Undefined
d. Undefined

159. In mathematics, _____ bear slight similarity to functions: they allow one to use arbitrary values, called parameters, in place of independent variables in equations, which in turn provide values for dependent variables. A simple kinematical example is when one uses a time parameter to determine the position, velocity, and other information about a body in motion.
   a. Thing
   b. Parametric equations0
   c. Undefined
   d. Undefined

160. In mathematics, a _____ is a rectangular table of numbers or, more generally, a table consisting of abstract quantities that can be added and multiplied.
   a. Matrix0
   b. Thing
   c. Undefined
   d. Undefined

161. Initial objects are also called _____, and terminal objects are also called final.
   a. Thing
   b. Coterminal0
   c. Undefined
   d. Undefined

162. In mathematics, a _____ is an ordered list of objects. Like a set, it contains members, also called elements or terms, and the number of terms is called the length of the _____. Unlike a set, order matters, and the exact same elements can appear multiple times at different positions in the _____.
   a. Thing
   b. Sequence0
   c. Undefined
   d. Undefined

Chapter 9. Conic Sections

1. In Euclidean geometry, a _____ is the set of all points in a plane at a fixed distance, called the radius, from a given point, the center.
   - a. Circle0
   - b. Thing
   - c. Undefined
   - d. Undefined

2. In mathematics, an _____ .
   - a. Ellipse0
   - b. Thing
   - c. Undefined
   - d. Undefined

3. In mathematics, the concept of a _____ tries to capture the intuitive idea of a geometrical one-dimensional and continuous object. A simple example is the circle.
   - a. Curve0
   - b. Thing
   - c. Undefined
   - d. Undefined

4. In mathematics, _____ are the intuitive idea of a geometrical one-dimensional and continuous object.
   - a. Curves0
   - b. Thing
   - c. Undefined
   - d. Undefined

5. In mathematics, the _____ is a conic section generated by the intersection of a right circular conical surface and a plane parallel to a generating straight line of that surface. It can also be defined as locus of points in a plane which are equidistant from a given point.
   - a. Thing
   - b. Parabola0
   - c. Undefined
   - d. Undefined

6. In mathematics, a _____ is a type of conic section defined as the intersection between a right circular conical surface and a plane which cuts through both halves of the cone.
   - a. Thing
   - b. Hyperbola0
   - c. Undefined
   - d. Undefined

7. In mathematics, a _____ section is a curve that can be formed by intersecting a cone with a plane.
   - a. Thing
   - b. Conic0
   - c. Undefined
   - d. Undefined

8. In mathematics, a _____ function in the sense of algebraic geometry is an everywhere-defined, polynomial function on an algebraic variety V with values in the field K over which V is defined.
   - a. Regular0
   - b. Thing
   - c. Undefined
   - d. Undefined

9. A _____, as defined by the International Astronomical Union , is a celestial body orbiting a star or stellar remnant that is massive enough to be rounded by its own gravity, not massive enough to cause thermonuclear fusion in its core, and has cleared its neighboring region of planetesimals.
   - a. Thing
   - b. Planet0
   - c. Undefined
   - d. Undefined

10. _____ is a set, with some particular properties and usually some additional structure, such as the operations of addition or multiplication, for instance.

a. Space0
b. Thing
c. Undefined
d. Undefined

11. _____ systems represent systems whose behavior is not expressible as a sum of the behaviors of its descriptors.
    a. Nonlinear0
    b. Thing
    c. Undefined
    d. Undefined

12. A _____ is a three-dimensional geometric shape formed by straight lines through a fixed point (vertex) to the points of a fixed curve (directrix)
    a. Concept
    b. Cone0
    c. Undefined
    d. Undefined

13. In mathematics, a _____ is a two-dimensional manifold or surface that is perfectly flat.
    a. Thing
    b. Plane0
    c. Undefined
    d. Undefined

14. In mathematics, the _____ of two sets A and B is the set that contains all elements of A that also belong to B (or equivalently, all elements of B that also belong to A), but no other elements.
    a. Intersection0
    b. Thing
    c. Undefined
    d. Undefined

15. In geometry, _____ lines are two lines that share one or more common points.
    a. Intersecting0
    b. Thing
    c. Undefined
    d. Undefined

16. A _____ is a set of numbers that designate location in a given reference system, such as x,y in a planar _____ system or an x,y,z in a three-dimensional _____ system.
    a. Thing
    b. Coordinate0
    c. Undefined
    d. Undefined

17. A _____ (or shape) refers to the external two-dimensional outline, appearance or configuration of some thing - in contrast to the matter or content or substance of which it is composed.
    a. Thing
    b. Plane figure0
    c. Undefined
    d. Undefined

18. _____ is a relation in Euclidean geometry among the three sides of a right triangle.
    a. Thing
    b. Pythagorean Theorem0
    c. Undefined
    d. Undefined

19. In mathematics, a _____ is a statement that can be proved on the basis of explicitly stated or previously agreed assumptions.
    a. Thing
    b. Theorem0
    c. Undefined
    d. Undefined

Chapter 9. Conic Sections

20. A _____ is a unit of length, usually used to measure distance, in a number of different systems, including Imperial units, United States customary units and Norwegian/Swedish mil. Its size can vary from system to system, but in each is between 1 and 10 kilometers. In contemporary English contexts _____ refers to either:
   a. Thing
   b. Mile0
   c. Undefined
   d. Undefined

21. A frame of _____ is a particular perspective from which the universe is observed.
   a. Reference0
   b. Thing
   c. Undefined
   d. Undefined

22. In mathematics, the _____ of a coordinate system is the point where the axes of the system intersect.
   a. Origin0
   b. Thing
   c. Undefined
   d. Undefined

23. _____ is the middle point of a line segment.
   a. Thing
   b. Midpoint0
   c. Undefined
   d. Undefined

24. In geometry, a line _____ is a part of a line that is bounded by two end points, and contains every point on the line between its end points.
   a. Segment0
   b. Concept
   c. Undefined
   d. Undefined

25. In geometry, an _____ is a point at which a line segment or ray terminates.
   a. Thing
   b. Endpoint0
   c. Undefined
   d. Undefined

26. In mathematics, an _____, mean, or central tendency of a data set refers to a measure of the "middle" or "expected" value of the data set.
   a. Concept
   b. Average0
   c. Undefined
   d. Undefined

27. A _____ is a part of a line that is bounded by two end points, and contains every point on the line between its end points.
   a. Thing
   b. Line segment0
   c. Undefined
   d. Undefined

28. In geometry, the _____ of an object is a point in some sense in the middle of the object.
   a. Thing
   b. Center0
   c. Undefined
   d. Undefined

29. In geometry, a _____ (Greek words diairo = divide and metro = measure) of a circle is any straight line segment that passes through the centre and whose endpoints are on the circular boundary, or, in more modern usage, the length of such a line segment. When using the word in the more modern sense, one speaks of the _____ rather than a _____, because all diameters of a circle have the same length. This length is twice the radius. The _____ of a circle is also the longest chord that the circle has.

a. Diameter0
b. Thing
c. Undefined
d. Undefined

30. In classical geometry, a _____ of a circle or sphere is any line segment from its center to its boundary. By extension, the _____ of a circle or sphere is the length of any such segment. The _____ is half the diameter. In science and engineering the term _____ of curvature is commonly used as a synonym for _____.
   a. Thing
   b. Radius0
   c. Undefined
   d. Undefined

31. The _____ is the distance around a closed curve. _____ is a kind of perimeter.
   a. Circumference0
   b. Thing
   c. Undefined
   d. Undefined

32. The _____ of measurement are a globally standardized and modernized form of the metric system.
   a. Units0
   b. Thing
   c. Undefined
   d. Undefined

33. In plane geometry, a _____ is a polygon with four equal sides, four right angles, and parallel opposite sides. In algebra, the _____ of a number is that number multiplied by itself.
   a. Thing
   b. Square0
   c. Undefined
   d. Undefined

34. Three or more points that lie on the same line are called _____.
   a. Thing
   b. Collinear0
   c. Undefined
   d. Undefined

35. A _____ is one of the basic shapes of geometry: a polygon with three vertices and three sides which are straight line segments.
   a. Thing
   b. Triangle0
   c. Undefined
   d. Undefined

36. In geometry, a _____ is a special kind of point, usually a corner of a polygon, polyhedron, or higher dimensional polytope. In the geometry of curves a _____ is a point of where the first derivative of curvature is zero. In graph theory, a _____ is the fundamental unit out of which graphs are formed
   a. Vertex0
   b. Thing
   c. Undefined
   d. Undefined

37. In geometry, an _____ polygon is a polygon which has all sides of the same length.
   a. Thing
   b. Equilateral0
   c. Undefined
   d. Undefined

38. _____ is the study of geometry using the principles of algebra. _____ can be explained more simply: it is concerned with defining geometrical shapes in a numerical way and extracting numerical information from that representation.

Chapter 9. Conic Sections

    a. Thing
    b. Analytic geometry0
    c. Undefined
    d. Undefined

39. An _____ triange is a triangle with at least two sides of equal length.
    a. Thing
    b. Isosceles0
    c. Undefined
    d. Undefined

40. In a _____ triangle, all sides have different lengths. The internal angles in a _____ triangle are all different.
    a. Scalene0
    b. Thing
    c. Undefined
    d. Undefined

41. In geometry, two lines or planes if one falls on the other in such a way as to create congruent adjacent angles. The term may be used as a noun or adjective. Thus, referring to Figure 1, the line AB is the _____ to CD through the point B.
    a. Perpendicular0
    b. Thing
    c. Undefined
    d. Undefined

42. _____ is a notation for writing numbers that is often used by scientists and mathematicians to make it easier to write large and small numbers.
    a. Thing
    b. Scientific notation0
    c. Undefined
    d. Undefined

43. _____ is a technique used in algebra to solve quadratic equations, in analytic geometry for determining the shapes of graphs, and in calculus for computing integrals, including, but hardly limited to, the integrals that define Laplace transforms. The essential objective is to reduce a quadratic polynomial in a variable in an equation or expression to a squared polynomial of linear order. This can reduce an equation or integral to one that is more easily solved or evaluated.
    a. Completing the square0
    b. Thing
    c. Undefined
    d. Undefined

44. A quadratic equation with real solutions, called roots, which may be real or complex, is given by the _____: $x = \frac{-b \pm \sqrt{b^2 - 4ac}}{2a}$.
    a. Quadratic formula0
    b. Thing
    c. Undefined
    d. Undefined

45. In mathematics, _____ allows the rapid division of any polynomial by a binomial of the form x − r. It was described by Paolo Ruffini in 1809. _____ is a special case of long division when the divisor is a linear factor.
    a. Ruffini's rule0
    b. Thing
    c. Undefined
    d. Undefined

46. _____ are activities that are governed by a set of rules or customs and often engaged in competitively.
    a. Sports0
    b. Thing
    c. Undefined
    d. Undefined

47. A _____, known as a parabolic dish or a parabolic mirror, is a reflective device, commonly formed in the shape of a paraboloid of revolution.

a. Parabolic reflector0
b. Thing
c. Undefined
d. Undefined

48. _____ means "constancy", i.e. if something retains a certain feature even after we change a way of looking at it, then it is symmetric.
   a. Symmetry0
   b. Thing
   c. Undefined
   d. Undefined

49. An _____ is a straight line around which a geometric figure can be rotated.
   a. Axis0
   b. Thing
   c. Undefined
   d. Undefined

50. _____ of a two-dimensional figure is a line such that, if a perpendicular is constructed, any two points lying on the perpendicular at equal distances from the _____ are identical.
   a. Thing
   b. Axis of symmetry0
   c. Undefined
   d. Undefined

51. The _____ of a ring R is defined to be the smallest positive integer n such that $n\, a = 0$, for all a in R.
   a. Thing
   b. Characteristic0
   c. Undefined
   d. Undefined

52. _____ are procedures that allow people to exchange information by one of several methods.
   a. Thing
   b. Communications0
   c. Undefined
   d. Undefined

53. In geometry, a _____ is the intersection of a body in 2-dimensional space with a line, or of a body in 3-dimensional space with a plane
   a. Cross section0
   b. Thing
   c. Undefined
   d. Undefined

54. In Euclidean geometry, a _____ is moving every point a constant distance in a specified direction.
   a. Concept
   b. Translation0
   c. Undefined
   d. Undefined

55. A _____ is a statement or claimt that a particular event will occur in the future in more certain terms than a forecast.
   a. Thing
   b. Prediction0
   c. Undefined
   d. Undefined

56. In astronomy, geography, geometry and related sciences and contexts, a plane is said to be _____ at a given point if it is locally perpendicular to the gradient of the gravity field, i.e., with the direction of the gravitational force at that point.
   a. Horizontal0
   b. Thing
   c. Undefined
   d. Undefined

57. In mathematics, a _____ in elementary terms is any of a variety of different functions from geometry, such as rotations, reflections and translations.

Chapter 9. Conic Sections

a. Thing
b. Transformation0
c. Undefined
d. Undefined

58. _____ is the transport of people on a trip/journey or the process or time involved in a person or object moving from one location to another.
a. Thing
b. Travel0
c. Undefined
d. Undefined

59. The Yakovlev Yak-25, NATO designation _____-A / Mandrake, was a swept wing, turbojet-powered interceptor aircraft and reconnaissance aircraft used by the Soviet Union.
a. Flashlight0
b. Thing
c. Undefined
d. Undefined

60. An _____ is a combination of numbers, operators, grouping symbols and/or free variables and bound variables arranged in a meaningful way which can be evaluated..
a. Expression0
b. Thing
c. Undefined
d. Undefined

61. In mathematics, a _____ number is a number which can be expressed as a ratio of two integers. Non-integer _____ numbers (commonly called fractions) are usually written as the vulgar fraction a / b, where b is not zero.
a. Rational0
b. Thing
c. Undefined
d. Undefined

62. In mathematics, a _____ is a mathematical statement which appears likely to be true, but has not been formally proven to be true under the rules of mathematical logic.
a. Conjecture0
b. Concept
c. Undefined
d. Undefined

63. In mathematics and the mathematical sciences, a _____ is a fixed, but possibly unspecified, value. This is in contrast to a variable, which is not fixed.
a. Thing
b. Constant0
c. Undefined
d. Undefined

64. In mathematics, an _____ is a statement about the relative size or order of two objects.
a. Thing
b. Inequality0
c. Undefined
d. Undefined

65. Acid _____ ratio measures the ability of a company to use its near cash or quick assets to immediately extinguish its current liabilities.
a. Test0
b. Thing
c. Undefined
d. Undefined

66. An _____ is the result from the sudden release of stored energy in the Earth's crust that creates seismic waves.
a. Earthquake0
b. Thing
c. Undefined
d. Undefined

Chapter 9. Conic Sections

67. The mathematical concept of a _____ expresses the intuitive idea of deterministic dependence between two quantities, one of which is viewed as primary and the other as secondary. A _____ then is a way to associate a unique output for each input of a specified type, for example, a real number or an element of a given set.
   a. Function0
   b. Thing
   c. Undefined
   d. Undefined

68. In geometry, the _____ are a pair of special points used in describing conic sections. The four types of conic sections are the circle, parabola, ellipse, and hyperbola.
   a. Foci0
   b. Thing
   c. Undefined
   d. Undefined

69. In linear algebra, a _____ of a matrix A is the determinant of some smaller square matrix, cut down from A.
   a. Minor0
   b. Thing
   c. Undefined
   d. Undefined

70. An _____ is when two lines intersect somewhere on a plane creating a right angle at intersection
   a. Axes0
   b. Thing
   c. Undefined
   d. Undefined

71. In physics, an _____ is the path that an object makes around another object while under the influence of a source of centripetal force, such as gravity.
   a. Thing
   b. Orbit0
   c. Undefined
   d. Undefined

72. In mathematics, _____ is a part of the set theoretic notion of function.
   a. Thing
   b. Image0
   c. Undefined
   d. Undefined

73. A _____ is a function that assigns a number to subsets of a given set.
   a. Measure0
   b. Thing
   c. Undefined
   d. Undefined

74. _____ is a parameter associated with every conic section.
   a. Eccentricity0
   b. Thing
   c. Undefined
   d. Undefined

75. A _____ is a quantity that denotes the proportional amount or magnitude of one quantity relative to another.
   a. Ratio0
   b. Thing
   c. Undefined
   d. Undefined

76. _____ is the scientific study of celestial objects such as stars, planets, comets, and galaxies; and phenomena that originate outside the Earth's atmosphere.
   a. Astronomy0
   b. Thing
   c. Undefined
   d. Undefined

77. A _____ is a unit of length in the metric system, equal to one thousand metres, the current SI base unit of length

Chapter 9. Conic Sections

a. Kilometer0
b. Thing
c. Undefined
d. Undefined

78. The National _____ is an area in the United States Capitol devoted to statues of people and symbols important in American history.
   a. Thing
   b. Statuary Hall0
   c. Undefined
   d. Undefined

79. A _____ is a gallery beneath a dome or vault or enclosed in a circular or elliptical area in which whispers can be heard clearly in other parts of the building.
   a. Whispering gallery0
   b. Thing
   c. Undefined
   d. Undefined

80. _____ is the art and science of designing buildings and structures.
   a. Architecture0
   b. Thing
   c. Undefined
   d. Undefined

81. In mathematics, a _____ (also spelled reflexion) is a map that transforms an object into its mirror image.
   a. Reflection0
   b. Concept
   c. Undefined
   d. Undefined

82. _____ is electromagnetic radiation with a wavelength that is visible to the eye (visible _____) or, in a technical or scientific context, electromagnetic radiation of any wavelength.
   a. Thing
   b. Light0
   c. Undefined
   d. Undefined

83. A _____ is a symbolic representation denoting a quantity or expression. It often represents an "unknown" quantity that has the potential to change.
   a. Thing
   b. Variable0
   c. Undefined
   d. Undefined

84. _____ is the logarithm to the base e, where e is an irrational constant approximately equal to 2.718281828459.
   a. Natural logarithm0
   b. Thing
   c. Undefined
   d. Undefined

85. In mathematics, a _____ of a number x is the exponent y of the power by such that $x = b^y$. The value used for the base b must be neither 0 nor 1, nor a root of 1 in the case of the extension to complex numbers, and is typically 10, e, or 2.
   a. Logarithm0
   b. Thing
   c. Undefined
   d. Undefined

86. A _____ is the result of the addition of a set of numbers. The numbers may be natural numbers, complex numbers, matrices, or still more complicated objects. An infinite _____ is a subtle procedure known as a series.
   a. Sum0
   b. Thing
   c. Undefined
   d. Undefined

Chapter 9. Conic Sections

87. In mathematics, a _____ is an expression that is constructed from one or more variables and constants, using only the operations of addition, subtraction, multiplication, and constant positive whole number exponents. is a _____. Note in particular that division by an expression containing a variable is not in general allowed in polynomials. [1]
   a. Thing
   b. Polynomial0
   c. Undefined
   d. Undefined

88. A _____ decimal is a number whose decimal representation eventually becomes periodic (i.e. the same number sequence _____ indefinitely).
   a. Repeating0
   b. Thing
   c. Undefined
   d. Undefined

89. _____ is the process of planning, recording, and controlling the movement of a craft or vehicle from one place to another.
   a. Thing
   b. Navigation0
   c. Undefined
   d. Undefined

90. In mathematics, the conjugate _____ or adjoint matrix of an m-by-n matrix A with complex entries is the n-by-m matrix A* obtained from A by taking the transpose and then taking the complex conjugate of each entry.
   a. Thing
   b. Pairs0
   c. Undefined
   d. Undefined

91. In mathematics, the _____ (or modulus) of a real number is its numerical value without regard to its sign.
   a. Thing
   b. Absolute value0
   c. Undefined
   d. Undefined

92. In algebra, a _____ is a binomial formed by taking the opposite of the second term of a binomial.
   a. Conjugate0
   b. Thing
   c. Undefined
   d. Undefined

93. In geometry, a _____ is defined as a quadrilateral where all four of its angles are right angles.
   a. Rectangle0
   b. Thing
   c. Undefined
   d. Undefined

94. A _____ can refer to a line joining two nonadjacent vertices of a polygon or polyhedron, or in some contexts any upward or downward sloping line. .
   a. Diagonal0
   b. Thing
   c. Undefined
   d. Undefined

95. A _____ is a negotiable instrument instructing a financial institution to pay a specific amount of a specific currency from a specific demand account held in the maker/depositor's name with that institution. Both the maker and payee may be natural persons or legal entities.
   a. Check0
   b. Thing
   c. Undefined
   d. Undefined

Chapter 9. Conic Sections

96. An _____ is a straight line or curve A to which another curve B approaches closer and closer as one moves along it. As one moves along B, the space between it and the _____ A becomes smaller and smaller, and can in fact be made as small as one could wish by going far enough along. A curve may or may not touch or cross its _____. In fact, the curve may intersect the _____ an infinite number of times.
- a. Thing
- b. Asymptote0
- c. Undefined
- d. Undefined

97. The metre (or _____, see spelling differences) is a measure of length. It is the basic unit of length in the metric system and in the International System of Units (SI), used around the world for general and scientific purposes.
- a. Concept
- b. Meter0
- c. Undefined
- d. Undefined

98. _____ are the basic objects of study in graph theory. Informally speaking, a graph is a set of objects called points, nodes, or vertices connected by links called lines or edges.
- a. Thing
- b. Graphs0
- c. Undefined
- d. Undefined

99. In mathematics, a _____ is the result of multiplying, or an expression that identifies factors to be multiplied.
- a. Product0
- b. Thing
- c. Undefined
- d. Undefined

100. Mathematical _____ really refers to two distinct areas of research: the first is the application of the techniques of formal _____ to mathematics and mathematical reasoning, and the second, in the other direction, the application of mathematical techniques to the representation and analysis of formal _____.
- a. Logic0
- b. Thing
- c. Undefined
- d. Undefined

101. A _____ is 360° or 2∂ radians.
- a. Turn0
- b. Thing
- c. Undefined
- d. Undefined

102. A _____ signifies a point or points of probability on a subject e.g., the _____ of creativity, which allows for the formation of rule or norm or law by interpretation of the phenomena events that can be created.
- a. Principle0
- b. Thing
- c. Undefined
- d. Undefined

103. Statistical _____ is a statistical procedure in which individual items are placed into groups based on quantitative information on one or more characteristics inherent in the items and based on a training set of previously labeled items.
- a. Classification0
- b. Thing
- c. Undefined
- d. Undefined

104. _____ is a physical property of a system that underlies the common notions of hot and cold; something that is hotter has the greater _____.
- a. Thing
- b. Temperature0
- c. Undefined
- d. Undefined

Chapter 9. Conic Sections

105. In mathematics, a matrix can be thought of as each row or _____ being a vector. Hence, a space formed by row vectors or _____ vectors are said to be a row space or a _____ space.
   a. Column0
   b. Concept
   c. Undefined
   d. Undefined

106. _____ are a set of equations containing multiple variables.
   a. Systems of equations0
   b. Thing
   c. Undefined
   d. Undefined

107. In mathematics, there are several meanings of _____ depending on the subject.
   a. Thing
   b. Degree0
   c. Undefined
   d. Undefined

108. The word _____ comes from the Latin word linearis, which means created by lines.
   a. Thing
   b. Linear0
   c. Undefined
   d. Undefined

109. A _____ represents a system whose behavior is not expressible as a sum of the behaviors of its descriptors.
   a. Nonlinear system0
   b. Thing
   c. Undefined
   d. Undefined

110. _____ is the estimation of a physical quantity such as distance, energy, temperature, or time.
   a. Thing
   b. Measurement0
   c. Undefined
   d. Undefined

111. The Gaussian _____ is an algorithm which can be used to determine the solutions of a system of linear equations, to find the rank of a matrix, and to calculate the inverse of an invertible square matrix.
   a. Thing
   b. Elimination method0
   c. Undefined
   d. Undefined

112. _____ is the art, science, and practice of studying and managing forests and plantations, and related natural resources.
   a. Forestry0
   b. Thing
   c. Undefined
   d. Undefined

113. The _____ is used to discard one of the variables in an equation, only to replace it with the actual value when solving multiple equations.
   a. Thing
   b. Substitution method0
   c. Undefined
   d. Undefined

114. A _____ is a number that is less than zero.
   a. Thing
   b. Negative number0
   c. Undefined
   d. Undefined

115. The plus and _____ signs are mathematical symbols used to represent the notions of positive and negative as well as the operations of addition and subtraction.

Chapter 9. Conic Sections

    a. Thing
    b. Minus0
    c. Undefined
    d. Undefined

116. In mathematics, a _____ is a rectangular table of numbers or, more generally, a table consisting of abstract quantities that can be added and multiplied.
    a. Thing
    b. Matrix0
    c. Undefined
    d. Undefined

117. _____ is a business term for the amount of money that a company receives from its activities in a given period, mostly from sales of products and/or services to customers
    a. Thing
    b. Revenue0
    c. Undefined
    d. Undefined

118. _____ is the application of tools and a processing medium to the transformation of raw materials into finished goods for sale.
    a. Thing
    b. Manufacturing0
    c. Undefined
    d. Undefined

119. _____ is the symbold used to indicate the nth root of a number
    a. Thing
    b. Radical0
    c. Undefined
    d. Undefined

120. _____, Greek for "knowledge of nature," is the branch of science concerned with the discovery and characterization of universal laws which govern matter, energy, space, and time.
    a. Thing
    b. Physics0
    c. Undefined
    d. Undefined

121. _____ is a kind of property which exists as magnitude or multitude. It is among the basic classes of things along with quality, substance, change, and relation.
    a. Thing
    b. Amount0
    c. Undefined
    d. Undefined

122. The _____, in practice often shortened to amp, is a unit of electric current, or amount of electric charge per second.
    a. Thing
    b. Amperes0
    c. Undefined
    d. Undefined

123. _____ has many meanings, most of which simply .
    a. Thing
    b. Power0
    c. Undefined
    d. Undefined

124. _____ was a German Lutheran mathematician, astronomer and astrologer, and a key figure in the 17th century astronomical revolution.
    a. Johannes Kepler0
    b. Person
    c. Undefined
    d. Undefined

Chapter 9. Conic Sections

125. A _____ is an abstract model that uses mathematical language to describe the behavior of a system. Eykhoff defined a _____ as 'a representation of the essential aspects of an existing system which presents knowledge of that system in usable form'.
   a. Mathematical model0
   b. Thing
   c. Undefined
   d. Undefined

126. In mathematics, the additive inverse, or _____ of a number n is the number that, when added to n, yields zero. The additive inverse of n is denoted −n. For example, 7 is −7, because 7 + (−7) = 0, and the additive inverse of −0.3 is 0.3, because −0.3 + 0.3 = 0.
   a. Thing
   b. Opposite0
   c. Undefined
   d. Undefined

127. In mathematics, the _____ of a number n is the number that, when added to n, yields zero. The _____ of n is denoted −n. For example, 7 is −7, because 7 + (−7) = 0, and the _____ of −0.3 is 0.3, because −0.3 + 0.3 = 0.
   a. Additive inverse0
   b. Thing
   c. Undefined
   d. Undefined

128. _____ is often used to describe the measurement of the steepness, incline, gradient, or grade of a straight line. The _____ is defined as the ratio of the "rise" divided by the "run" between two points on a line, or in other words, the ratio of the altitude change to the horizontal distance between any two points on the line.
   a. Slope0
   b. Thing
   c. Undefined
   d. Undefined

129. In algebra, a _____ is a function depending on n that associates a scalar, det(A), to every $n \times n$ square matrix A.
   a. Thing
   b. Determinant0
   c. Undefined
   d. Undefined

130. A _____ is a polynomial function of the form f(x) = ax^2 + bx +c , where a, b, c are real numbers and a , 0.
   a. Quadratic function0
   b. Event
   c. Undefined
   d. Undefined

131. In mathematics, a _____ is an ordered list of objects. Like a set, it contains members, also called elements or terms, and the number of terms is called the length of the _____. Unlike a set, order matters, and the exact same elements can appear multiple times at different positions in the _____.
   a. Sequence0
   b. Thing
   c. Undefined
   d. Undefined

Chapter 10. Discrete Mathematics: Counting Principles and Probability

1. The outcome of a trial is called the _____.
   a. ADE classification
   b. Event10
   c. Undefined
   d. Undefined

2. A _____ provides a quantitative description of the likely occurrence of a particular event. _____ is conventionally expressed on a scale from 0 to 1; a rare event has a _____ close to 0, a very common event has a _____ close to 1. _____ is calculated as the ratio of the number of favorable events to the total number of possible events.
   a. Probability10
   b. -equivalence
   c. Undefined
   d. Undefined

3. A _____ is a well-defined collection of objects considered as a whole.
   a. -equivalence
   b. Set10
   c. Undefined
   d. Undefined

4. _____, or less commonly, denary, usually refers to the base 10 numeral system.
   a. -equivalence
   b. Decimal10
   c. Undefined
   d. Undefined

5. A _____ is a quotient of numbers, like 3⁄4, or more generally, an element of a quotient field.
   a. Fraction10
   b. -equivalence
   c. Undefined
   d. Undefined

6. A percentage is a way of expressing a proportion, a ratio or a fraction as a whole number, by using 100 as the denominator. A number such as "45%" ("45 percent" or "45 per cent") is shorthand for the fraction 45/100 or 0.45. As an illustration,"45 _____ of human beings..." is equivalent to both of the following:"45 out of every 100 people..." "0.45 of the human population..." One way to think about percentages is to realize that "one percent", represented by the symbol %, is simply the number 1/100, or 0.01.
   a. -equivalence
   b. Percent10
   c. Undefined
   d. Undefined

7. An _____ is any process or study, which results in the collection of data, the outcome of which is unknown. In statistics, the term is usually restricted to situations in which the researcher has control over some of the conditions under which the _____ takes place.
   a. ADE classification
   b. Experiment10
   c. Undefined
   d. Undefined

8. A _____ is a subset or portion of a population. Samples are extremely important in the field of statistical analysis, since due to economic and practical constraints we usually cannot make measurements on every single member of the particular population.
   a. Sample10
   b. -equivalence
   c. Undefined
   d. Undefined

9. The _____ is an exhaustive list of all the possible outcomes of an experiment. Each possible result of such a study is represented by one and only one point in the _____, which is usually denoted by S.

a. -equivalence
b. Sample Space10
c. Undefined
d. Undefined

10. In a large distribution of data it is often easier to understand the data if it is grouped into intervals where each _____ can contain more than one data value. Distributions are often reduced to 10 to 20 intervals.
   a. ADE classification
   b. Interval10
   c. Undefined
   d. Undefined

11. At times we must contend with variables that assume a large number of values. In this case it is typical to create _____ of values of the variable and then make a frequency tally of the number of observations falling within each interval. As is the case with any data reduction technique, detail is lost.
   a. ADE classification
   b. Intervals10
   c. Undefined
   d. Undefined

12. A _____ is an undefined term. However, it is often thought of as a series of points. A _____ has one dimension - length. A _____ is either named by a lower case letter or by two points on the _____.
   a. -equivalence
   b. Line10
   c. Undefined
   d. Undefined

13. A _____ is an undefined term. We usually represent this by a dot, but a _____ actually has no dimension. A capital letter names any _____.
   a. -equivalence
   b. Point10
   c. Undefined
   d. Undefined

14. The frequency of occurrence of one event divided by the frequency of occurrence of another event gives us the _____. For example, the frequency of success divided by the frequency of failure.
   a. Odds10
   b. ADE classification
   c. Undefined
   d. Undefined

15. A _____ is a relation where every x value has one and only y value.
   a. -equivalence
   b. Function10
   c. Undefined
   d. Undefined

16. An _____ is an indication of the value of an unknown quantity based on observed data. More formally, an _____ is the particular value of an estimator that is obtained from a particular sample of data and used to indicate the value of a parameter.
   a. ADE classification
   b. Estimate10
   c. Undefined
   d. Undefined

17. A _____ is a scheme for the numerical representation of the values of a variable. The interpretation we place upon the numbers of the _____, rather than the numbers themselves, makes the _____ useful. The most common scales are nominal, ordinal, interval
   a. Scale10
   b. -equivalence
   c. Undefined
   d. Undefined

Chapter 10. Discrete Mathematics: Counting Principles and Probability

18. The most important measure of central tendency, and one of the basic building blocks of all statistical analysis, is the arithmetic _____. It is simply the sum of all the set of values divided by the number of values involved. It can also be called the average.
   a. Mean10
   b. -equivalence
   c. Undefined
   d. Undefined

19. A _____ is a number or variable, or the product or quotient of a number or variable.
   a. Term10
   b. -equivalence
   c. Undefined
   d. Undefined

20. _____ refer to any data source, whether individuals, physical or biological things, geographic locations, time periods, or events; that is, anything upon which observations can be made.
   a. Objects10
   b. ADE classification
   c. Undefined
   d. Undefined

21. An _____ combines numbers, operators, and/or variables but contains no equal or inequality sign.
   a. Expression10
   b. ADE classification
   c. Undefined
   d. Undefined

22. _____ (from the Greek words Geo = earth and metro = measure) is the branch of mathematics first popularized in ancient Greek culture by Thales (circa 624-547 BC) dealing with spatial relationships. The earliest beginnings of _____ may be traced to Ancient Egypt
   a. -equivalence
   b. Geometry10
   c. Undefined
   d. Undefined

23. A _____ is the point that occurs whenever two lines, line segments, or rays meet. The _____ of an angle is very important.
   a. Vertex10
   b. -equivalence
   c. Undefined
   d. Undefined

24. _____ consist of the positive natural numbers (1, 2, 3, ...), their negatives (−1, −2, −3, ...) and the number zero.
   a. ADE classification
   b. Integers10
   c. Undefined
   d. Undefined

25. By a _____ we mean that every member of a population has an equal chance of being included in the sample; more strictly, every possible sample of the specified size has an equal chance of being selected from the population.
   a. Random sample10
   b. -equivalence
   c. Undefined
   d. Undefined

26. _____ is the study of quantity, structure, space, and change. Historically, _____ developed from counting, calculation, measurement, and the study of the shapes and motions of physical objects, through the use of abstraction and deductive reasoning.
   a. -equivalence
   b. Mathematics10
   c. Undefined
   d. Undefined

Chapter 10. Discrete Mathematics: Counting Principles and Probability

27. Two events are _____ when the occurrence of one precludes the occurrence of the other. Another word for _____ is disjoint.
   a. -equivalence
   b. Mutually exclusive10
   c. Undefined
   d. Undefined

28. Addition (or summation) is one of the basic operations of arithmetic. In its simplest form, addition combines two numbers, the augend and addend, into a single number, the _____. Adding more numbers can be viewed as repeated addition. (Repeated addition of the number one is the most basic form of counting.) By extension, the addition of zero numbers, one number, or infinitely many numbers can be defined.
   a. Sum10
   b. -equivalence
   c. Undefined
   d. Undefined

29. _____ states that two events are mutually exclusive (or disjoint) if it is impossible for them to occur together.
   a. -equivalence
   b. Mutually Exclusive Events10
   c. Undefined
   d. Undefined

30. Any number that is divisible by 2 is an _____ number.
   a. Even10
   b. ADE classification
   c. Undefined
   d. Undefined

31. _____ (or summation) is one of the basic operations of arithmetic. In its simplest form, _____ combines two numbers, the augend and addend, into a single number, the sum.
   a. ADE classification
   b. Addition10
   c. Undefined
   d. Undefined

32. A quadrilateral with 4 equal sides and all right angles is called a _____.
   a. Square10
   b. -equivalence
   c. Undefined
   d. Undefined

33. A _____ is a series of points the same distance from a given point, called the center.
   a. -equivalence
   b. Circle10
   c. Undefined
   d. Undefined

34. An _____ is represented by two expressions that have the same value.
   a. Equation10
   b. ADE classification
   c. Undefined
   d. Undefined

35. We have _____ when the occurrence of one has no effect on the probability of the occurrence of the other.
   a. Independent events10
   b. ADE classification
   c. Undefined
   d. Undefined

36. An _____ is the result of an experiment or other situation involving uncertainty.
   a. ADE classification
   b. Outcome10
   c. Undefined
   d. Undefined

37. The highest number in a list of values is called the _____.

Chapter 10. Discrete Mathematics: Counting Principles and Probability   143

   a. -equivalence
   c. Undefined
   b. Maximum10
   d. Undefined

38. The lowest number in a list of values is called the _____.
   a. Minimum10
   c. Undefined
   b. -equivalence
   d. Undefined

39. The graph of a quadrataic equation is a symmetric curve called a _____.
   a. Parabola10
   c. Undefined
   b. -equivalence
   d. Undefined

40. A _____ is a concrete example of an item or a specification against which all others may be measured. For example, there are "primary standards" for length, mass (see Kilogram standard), and other units of measure, kept by laboratories and standards organizations.
   a. -equivalence
   c. Undefined
   b. Standard10
   d. Undefined

41. The probability of one event given the occurrence of some other event is a _____.
   a. -equivalence
   c. Undefined
   b. Conditional probability10
   d. Undefined

42. _____ is any number that multiples to get a product..
   a. Factor10
   c. Undefined
   b. -equivalence
   d. Undefined

43. The _____ of a graph or equation is the set of all the possible x values.
   a. -equivalence
   c. Undefined
   b. Domain10
   d. Undefined

44. A _____ is a class of simple functions where they are constructed using only multiplication and addition of terms.
   a. Polynomial10
   c. Undefined
   b. -equivalence
   d. Undefined

45. A _____ contains at least one squared term.
   a. -equivalence
   c. Undefined
   b. Quadratic10
   d. Undefined

46. _____ refers to taking a root of a number. _____ 16 means to find the square root of 16, which is 4.
   a. -equivalence
   c. Undefined
   b. Radical10
   d. Undefined

47. The _____ is often confused with the median. The Median is a statistic for the distribution whereas the _____ provides a statistic for an interval; it is the center of the interval; the arithmetic average of the upper and lower limits.

a. -equivalence
b. Midpoint10
c. Undefined
d. Undefined

48. The word _____ can have three meanings: In _____ theory, a _____ is an abstract object consisting of vertices (or nodes) and edges (or arcs) between pairs of vertices. The _____ of a function f : X ¨ Y is the set of all pairs (x,f(x)) The _____ of a relation, a generalisation of the _____ of a function.
 a. Graph10
 b. -equivalence
 c. Undefined
 d. Undefined

49. A _____ is the relationship between two quantities. It is expressed as the quotient of two numbers, or as two numbers separated by a colon (pronounced "to"). A number that can be written as a _____ of two integers is a rational number.
 a. Ratio10
 b. -equivalence
 c. Undefined
 d. Undefined

50. The _____ or central tendency of a list of n numbers. All the values are added together and then divided by the number of values. It is also call the mean..
 a. Average10
 b. ADE classification
 c. Undefined
 d. Undefined

51. The goal of most inferential statistical analyses is to be able to generalize or apply the findings to the entire population and not just to the sample. The concept of _____ requires that the researcher determine some level of probability that the findings were due to chance or that they actually describe the population. The value of the probability that the findings were due to chance is usually reported when the findings of an analysis is reported.
 a. -equivalence
 b. Generalization10
 c. Undefined
 d. Undefined

52. Parallel is a term in geometry and in everyday life that refers to a property in Euclidean space of two or more lines or planes, or a combination of these. The existence and properties of _____ are the basis of Euclid's parallel postulate. As shown by the tick marks, lines a and b are parallel. We can prove this because the transversal t produces congruent angles.When lines or planes are parallel, then every point on one is located exactly the same minimum distance from the other line or plane. Another way of defining it is that any two _____ or planes, if extended to infinity in both directions, will never intersect. This second definition carries the condition that the extension must occur only in one additional dimension: In other words, _____ must be located in the same plane, and parallel planes must be located in the same three-dimensional space. A parallel combination of a line and a plane may be located in the same three-dimensional space. A third definition is: if two lines are both intersected by a third line (a transversal) in the same plane, and the angles of intersection are equal, then the two lines are parallel.
 a. Parallel lines10
 b. -equivalence
 c. Undefined
 d. Undefined

53. When 2 or more equations are considered as a group, this creates a _____.
 a. System of equations10
 b. -equivalence
 c. Undefined
 d. Undefined

54. Any time one number is on the left side of another number on a number line, the first number is _____ the second number. The symbol for this is <.

Chapter 10. Discrete Mathematics: Counting Principles and Probability

a. Less than10
b. -equivalence
c. Undefined
d. Undefined

55. By _____ we mean collecting observations made upon our environment -- observations, which are the results of measurements using clocks, balances, measuring rods, counting operations, or other objectively defined measuring instruments or procedures. _____ may mean simply counting the number of times a particular property occurs.
  a. Data10
  b. -equivalence
  c. Undefined
  d. Undefined

56. A _____, also referred to as a universe, is any well-defined collection of things. By well-defined we mean that the members of the _____ are spelled out, or an unequivocal statement is made as to which things belong in it and which do not.
  a. Population10
  b. -equivalence
  c. Undefined
  d. Undefined

57. A _____ is the answer in multiplication, or an expression that identifies factors to be multiplied
  a. -equivalence
  b. Product10
  c. Undefined
  d. Undefined

Chapter 11. Discrete Mathematics: Series and Patterns

1. _____ or arithmetics (from the Greek word áñéèìüò = number) in common usage is a branch of (or the forerunner of) mathematics which records elementary properties of certain operations on numerals, though in usage by professional mathematicians, it often is treated as a synonym for number theory.
   a. Arithmetic11
   b. ADE classification
   c. Undefined
   d. Undefined

2. A _____ is simply a polynomial with two terms such as this example: 2x + 7.
   a. -equivalence
   b. Binomial11
   c. Undefined
   d. Undefined

3. The _____ of a graph or equation is the set of all the possible x values.
   a. -equivalence
   b. Domain11
   c. Undefined
   d. Undefined

4. A _____ is a relation where every x value has one and only y value.
   a. -equivalence
   b. Function11
   c. Undefined
   d. Undefined

5. A _____ is a well-defined collection of objects considered as a whole.
   a. -equivalence
   b. Set11
   c. Undefined
   d. Undefined

6. A measure of variability, the _____ is the distance from the lowest to the highest score.
   a. Range11
   b. -equivalence
   c. Undefined
   d. Undefined

7. _____ are intuitively defined as numbers that are in one-to-one correspondence with the points on an infinite line—the number line. The term "real number" is a retronym coined in response to "imaginary number" _____ may be rational or irrational; algebraic or transcendental; and positive, negative, or zero _____ measure continuous quantities. They may in theory be expressed by decimal fractions that have an infinite sequence of digits to the right of the decimal point; these are often (mis-)represented in the same form as 324.823211247... (where the three dots express that there would still be more digits to come, no matter how many more might be added at the end).
   a. Real numbers11
   b. -equivalence
   c. Undefined
   d. Undefined

8. A _____ is a number or variable, or the product or quotient of a number or variable.
   a. -equivalence
   b. Term11
   c. Undefined
   d. Undefined

9. One major objective of statistical analysis is the identification of associations or _____ that exist between and among sets of observations. In other words, does knowledge about about one set of data allow us to infer or predict characteristics about another set or sets of data.
   a. Relationships11
   b. -equivalence
   c. Undefined
   d. Undefined

10. An _____ combines numbers, operators, and/or variables but contains no equal or inequality sign.

a. Expression11   b. ADE classification
c. Undefined   d. Undefined

11. Addition (or summation) is one of the basic operations of arithmetic. In its simplest form, addition combines two numbers, the augend and addend, into a single number, the _____. Adding more numbers can be viewed as repeated addition. (Repeated addition of the number one is the most basic form of counting.) By extension, the addition of zero numbers, one number, or infinitely many numbers can be defined.
   a. -equivalence   b. Sum11
   c. Undefined   d. Undefined

12. _____ is the property of multiplication over addition which demonstrates that for all numbers a,b,c; a(b+c)=ab+ac, and ab+ac=a(b+c).
   a. -equivalence   b. Distributive property11
   c. Undefined   d. Undefined

13. A number that does not change in value in a given situation is a _____.
   a. -equivalence   b. Constant11
   c. Undefined   d. Undefined

14. A _____ contains at least one squared term.
   a. -equivalence   b. Quadratic11
   c. Undefined   d. Undefined

15. _____ consist of the positive natural numbers (1, 2, 3, ...), their negatives (−1, −2, −3, ...) and the number zero.
   a. Integers11   b. ADE classification
   c. Undefined   d. Undefined

16. An _____ is composed of two rays that have a common endpoint, called the vertex. Each _____ is named by a lower case letter or by one point from each ray and the vertex inbetween. _____ a might be the same _____ as _____ ABC.
   a. ADE classification   b. Angle11
   c. Undefined   d. Undefined

17. _____ are used to measure the size of angles. A circle has 360 _____ in it.
   a. Degrees11   b. -equivalence
   c. Undefined   d. Undefined

18. _____ (from the Greek words Geo = earth and metro = measure) is the branch of mathematics first popularized in ancient Greek culture by Thales (circa 624-547 BC) dealing with spatial relationships. The earliest beginnings of _____ may be traced to Ancient Egypt
   a. -equivalence   b. Geometry11
   c. Undefined   d. Undefined

19. A closed shape whose sides are all line segments is called a _____.

a. Polygon11
b. -equivalence
c. Undefined
d. Undefined

20. The combination of a particular row and column; the set of observations obtained under identical treatment conditions is simply a _____.
   a. Cell11
   b. -equivalence
   c. Undefined
   d. Undefined

21. An _____ is represented by two expressions that have the same value.
   a. Equation11
   b. ADE classification
   c. Undefined
   d. Undefined

22. A _____ is an undefined term. However, it is often thought of as a series of points. A _____ has one dimension - length. A _____ is either named by a lower case letter or by two points on the _____.
   a. -equivalence
   b. Line11
   c. Undefined
   d. Undefined

23. A _____ is an undefined term. We usually represent this by a dot, but a _____ actually has no dimension. A capital letter names any _____.
   a. -equivalence
   b. Point11
   c. Undefined
   d. Undefined

24. The _____ is part of the quadratic formula used to determine the number and kind of solutions to that particular quadratic equation.
   a. -equivalence
   b. Discriminant11
   c. Undefined
   d. Undefined

25. When 2 or more equations are considered as a group, this creates a _____.
   a. -equivalence
   b. System of equations11
   c. Undefined
   d. Undefined

26. _____ is an estimate of the decrease in the value of an asset, caused by "wear and tear", obsolescence, or impairment. The use of _____ affects a company's (or an individual's) financial statements, and, in some countries, their taxes.
   a. Depreciation11
   b. -equivalence
   c. Undefined
   d. Undefined

27. The answer to subtraction is called the _____.
   a. Difference11
   b. -equivalence
   c. Undefined
   d. Undefined

28. Any set of ordered pairs is called a _____.
   a. -equivalence
   b. Relation11
   c. Undefined
   d. Undefined

Chapter 11. Discrete Mathematics: Series and Patterns

29. The word _____ can have three meanings: In _____ theory, a _____ is an abstract object consisting of vertices (or nodes) and edges (or arcs) between pairs of vertices. The _____ of a function f : X ¨ Y is the set of all pairs (x,f(x)) The _____ of a relation, a generalisation of the _____ of a function.
    a. Graph11
    b. -equivalence
    c. Undefined
    d. Undefined

30. In a proportion the "middle" values are often referred to as the _____.
    a. Means11
    b. -equivalence
    c. Undefined
    d. Undefined

31. A _____ is a number that when multiplied by a given number gives you one. This is also called multiplicative inverse.
    a. -equivalence
    b. Reciprocal11
    c. Undefined
    d. Undefined

32. The _____ or central tendency of a list of n numbers. All the values are added together and then divided by the number of values. It is also call the mean..
    a. Average11
    b. ADE classification
    c. Undefined
    d. Undefined

33. A _____ must contain a right angle.
    a. -equivalence
    b. Right triangle11
    c. Undefined
    d. Undefined

34. Any polygon that has 3 sides is called a _____.
    a. Triangle11
    b. -equivalence
    c. Undefined
    d. Undefined

35. A _____ is a series of points the same distance from a given point, called the center.
    a. -equivalence
    b. Circle11
    c. Undefined
    d. Undefined

36. A _____ is a concrete example of an item or a specification against which all others may be measured. For example, there are "primary standards" for length, mass (see Kilogram standard), and other units of measure, kept by laboratories and standards organizations.
    a. Standard11
    b. -equivalence
    c. Undefined
    d. Undefined

37. A _____ is a subset or portion of a population. Samples are extremely important in the field of statistical analysis, since due to economic and practical constraints we usually cannot make measurements on every single member of the particular population.
    a. -equivalence
    b. Sample11
    c. Undefined
    d. Undefined

38. _____ measures how heavy or light something is.

Chapter 11. Discrete Mathematics: Series and Patterns

  a. Weight11
  c. Undefined
  b. -equivalence
  d. Undefined

39. The first grouping symbol used are called _____ ( ).
  a. -equivalence
  c. Undefined
  b. Parentheses11
  d. Undefined

40. A _____ is a class of simple functions where they are constructed using only multiplication and addition of terms.
  a. Polynomial11
  c. Undefined
  b. -equivalence
  d. Undefined

41. A _____ is the answer in multiplication, or an expression that identifies factors to be multiplied
  a. Product11
  c. Undefined
  b. -equivalence
  d. Undefined

42. A quadrilateral with 4 equal sides and all right angles is called a _____.
  a. -equivalence
  c. Undefined
  b. Square11
  d. Undefined

43. A _____ is the relationship between two quantities. It is expressed as the quotient of two numbers, or as two numbers separated by a colon (pronounced "to"). A number that can be written as a _____ of two integers is a rational number.
  a. Ratio11
  c. Undefined
  b. -equivalence
  d. Undefined

44. Whenever you divide by zero the answer is _____.
  a. Undefined11
  c. Undefined
  b. ADE classification
  d. Undefined

45. A _____ is a positive integer (1,2,3,...).
  a. Natural number11
  c. Undefined
  b. -equivalence
  d. Undefined

46. _____ measure how long something is.
  a. Length11
  c. Undefined
  b. -equivalence
  d. Undefined

47. A triangle with all sides of equal length is called an _____.
  a. ADE classification
  c. Undefined
  b. Equilateral triangle11
  d. Undefined

48. _____, or less commonly, denary, usually refers to the base 10 numeral system.
  a. -equivalence
  c. Undefined
  b. Decimal11
  d. Undefined

49. Another word for independent variables in the analysis of variance is _____.

Chapter 11. Discrete Mathematics: Series and Patterns

    a. -equivalence
    c. Undefined
    b. Factors11
    d. Undefined

50. a _____ (or informally fraction) is a ratio or quotient of two integers, usually written as the fraction a/b, where b is not zero. Each _____ can be written in infinitely many forms, for example 3 / 6 = 2 / 4 = 1 / 2. When rational numbers are turned into the decimal equivalents the numbers eventually end or repeat.
    a. Rational number11
    c. Undefined
    b. -equivalence
    d. Undefined

51. A _____ is a quotient of numbers, like 3⁄4, or more generally, an element of a quotient field.
    a. Fraction11
    c. Undefined
    b. -equivalence
    d. Undefined

52. Sometimes, when a fraction is converted to a decimal, one or more digits occurs over and over. This is called a _____. One-third becomes .333333... and is an example of a _____.
    a. Repeating decimal11
    c. Undefined
    b. -equivalence
    d. Undefined

53. A _____ provides a quantitative description of the likely occurrence of a particular event. _____ is conventionally expressed on a scale from 0 to 1; a rare event has a _____ close to 0, a very common event has a _____ close to 1. _____ is calculated as the ratio of the number of favorable events to the total number of possible events.
    a. -equivalence
    c. Undefined
    b. Probability11
    d. Undefined

54. The outcome of a trial is called the _____.
    a. ADE classification
    c. Undefined
    b. Event11
    d. Undefined

55. An _____ is the result of an experiment or other situation involving uncertainty.
    a. Outcome11
    c. Undefined
    b. ADE classification
    d. Undefined

56. An _____ is any process or study, which results in the collection of data, the outcome of which is unknown. In statistics, the term is usually restricted to situations in which the researcher has control over some of the conditions under which the _____ takes place.
    a. ADE classification
    c. Undefined
    b. Experiment11
    d. Undefined

57. Two events are _____ when the occurrence of one precludes the occurrence of the other. Another word for _____ is disjoint.
    a. -equivalence
    c. Undefined
    b. Mutually exclusive11
    d. Undefined

58. A _____ displays information in rows and columns.

a. -equivalence
b. Chart11
c. Undefined
d. Undefined

59. By _____ we mean collecting observations made upon our environment -- observations, which are the results of measurements using clocks, balances, measuring rods, counting operations, or other objectively defined measuring instruments or procedures. _____ may mean simply counting the number of times a particular property occurs.
   a. -equivalence
   b. Data11
   c. Undefined
   d. Undefined

60. _____ is a quick way of adding identical numbers. For example, the sum 7 + 7 + 7 can be found by multiplying 3 times 7. This model is reflected in the use of the word times as a synonym for multiplied by. The resuult of multiplying numbers is called a product. The numbers being multiplied are called factors.
   a. Multiplication11
   b. -equivalence
   c. Undefined
   d. Undefined

61. Whenever a number is written in exponential expression, the exponent can also be called a _____.
   a. Power11
   b. -equivalence
   c. Undefined
   d. Undefined

62. _____ refer to any data source, whether individuals, physical or biological things, geographic locations, time periods, or events; that is, anything upon which observations can be made.
   a. ADE classification
   b. Objects11
   c. Undefined
   d. Undefined

63. When something occurs once a year it is said to occur _____.
   a. Annually11
   b. ADE classification
   c. Undefined
   d. Undefined

64. The amount of money paid for borrowing or investing money is called the _____. There are two main kinds of _____ called simple _____ and compound _____.
   a. ADE classification
   b. Interest11
   c. Undefined
   d. Undefined

65. Whenever a number is not divisible by 2, then it is called an _____ number.
   a. ADE classification
   b. Odd11
   c. Undefined
   d. Undefined

66. The _____ refers to the amount of change in Y for a 1 unit change in X or is the ratio of the rise over the run; or in-other-words, the rate of change in the predicted value as a function of a change in the predictor variable.
   a. -equivalence
   b. Slope11
   c. Undefined
   d. Undefined

67. _____ is any number that multiples to get a product..
   a. Factor11
   b. -equivalence
   c. Undefined
   d. Undefined

68. Since the observations in most data distributions tend to cluster heavily about certain values, one logical measure of central tendency would be that value which occurs most frequently; and that value is referred to as the _____ or modal value. For a nominal scale of measurement, the _____ is the best indicator of central tendency.
   a. -equivalence
   b. Mode11
   c. Undefined
   d. Undefined

Chapter 12. Discrete Mathematics: Statistics

1. By _____ we mean collecting observations made upon our environment -- observations, which are the results of measurements using clocks, balances, measuring rods, counting operations, or other objectively defined measuring instruments or procedures. _____ may mean simply counting the number of times a particular property occurs.
   a. -equivalence
   b. Data12
   c. Undefined
   d. Undefined

2. The associations uncovered by statistical analysis are basically of two types. One type is that the relationship identified between two sets of observations is purely _____ or "correlational" in nature, and no conclusions can be drawn about causality.
   a. Descriptive12
   b. -equivalence
   c. Undefined
   d. Undefined

3. An association or relationship in which we can be relatively confident that the variables are related in a causal manner are called _____ or experimental relationships. These are relationships in which we manipulate the levels of one variable and measure the effect.
   a. Inferential12
   b. ADE classification
   c. Undefined
   d. Undefined

4. Statistical analysis, sometimes referred to simply as _____, is concerned with the definition and collection, organization, and interpretation of data according to well-defined procedures. The term itself, _____, is a defining characteristic of a sample, such as a sample mean, or sample standard deviation.
   a. -equivalence
   b. Statistics12
   c. Undefined
   d. Undefined

5. A statistic describes some characteristic of a set of data. When these statistics are used to make decisions such as whether two independent sets of data should be considered as representing the same object or that they really represent two different objects, such statistics are referred to as _____ - fundamentally, helping making inferences whether things are the same or different.
   a. Inferential statistics12
   b. ADE classification
   c. Undefined
   d. Undefined

6. A _____, also referred to as a universe, is any well-defined collection of things. By well-defined we mean that the members of the _____ are spelled out, or an unequivocal statement is made as to which things belong in it and which do not.
   a. -equivalence
   b. Population12
   c. Undefined
   d. Undefined

7. A _____ is a subset or portion of a population. Samples are extremely important in the field of statistical analysis, since due to economic and practical constraints we usually cannot make measurements on every single member of the particular population.
   a. -equivalence
   b. Sample12
   c. Undefined
   d. Undefined

8. _____ refers to the process of selecting one or more samples of a population. Samples may be selected randomly or systematically.

a. Sampling12
b. -equivalence
c. Undefined
d. Undefined

9. A summary value that would suggest a typical or representative observation of a distribution of data, is a measure of _____ or location; that is, a value at which the observations tend to center.
a. Central tendency12
b. -equivalence
c. Undefined
d. Undefined

10. The most important measure of central tendency, and one of the basic building blocks of all statistical analysis, is the arithmetic _____. It is simply the sum of all the set of values divided by the number of values involved. It can also be called the average.
a. -equivalence
b. Mean12
c. Undefined
d. Undefined

11. A measure of central tendency, the _____, corresponds to the point having 50% of the observations below it when observations are arranged in numerical order. The _____ assumes at least an interval level of measurement. For a symmetric distribution such as the normal distribution, the _____ is the same as the mean. For a distribution which is skewed to the right, the _____ is typically smaller than the mean or when skewed to the left, the _____ is smaller.
a. Median12
b. -equivalence
c. Undefined
d. Undefined

12. Since the observations in most data distributions tend to cluster heavily about certain values, one logical measure of central tendency would be that value which occurs most frequently; and that value is referred to as the _____ or modal value. For a nominal scale of measurement, the _____ is the best indicator of central tendency.
a. Mode12
b. -equivalence
c. Undefined
d. Undefined

13. _____ or arithmetics (from the Greek word áñéèìüò = number) in common usage is a branch of (or the forerunner of) mathematics which records elementary properties of certain operations on numerals, though in usage by professional mathematicians, it often is treated as a synonym for number theory.
a. ADE classification
b. Arithmetic12
c. Undefined
d. Undefined

14. The _____ or central tendency of a list of n numbers. All the values are added together and then divided by the number of values. It is also call the mean..
a. Average12
b. ADE classification
c. Undefined
d. Undefined

15. A _____ is a well-defined collection of objects considered as a whole.
a. -equivalence
b. Set12
c. Undefined
d. Undefined

16. Addition (or summation) is one of the basic operations of arithmetic. In its simplest form, addition combines two numbers, the augend and addend, into a single number, the _____. Adding more numbers can be viewed as repeated addition. (Repeated addition of the number one is the most basic form of counting.) By extension, the addition of zero numbers, one number, or infinitely many numbers can be defined.

a. Sum12
b. -equivalence
c. Undefined
d. Undefined

17. Any number that is divisible by 2 is an _____ number.
   a. ADE classification
   b. Even12
   c. Undefined
   d. Undefined

18. A _____ distribution has two distinct peaks. The peaks correspond to the most frequently occurring scores or values in the distribution.
   a. -equivalence
   b. Bimodal12
   c. Undefined
   d. Undefined

19. The number of times a particular score or observation occurs is its _____.
   a. Frequency12
   b. -equivalence
   c. Undefined
   d. Undefined

20. An _____ is an indication of the value of an unknown quantity based on observed data. More formally, an _____ is the particular value of an estimator that is obtained from a particular sample of data and used to indicate the value of a parameter.
   a. ADE classification
   b. Estimate12
   c. Undefined
   d. Undefined

21. A percentage is a way of expressing a proportion, a ratio or a fraction as a whole number, by using 100 as the denominator. A number such as "45%" ("45 percent" or "45 per cent") is shorthand for the fraction 45/100 or 0.45. As an illustration, "45 _____ of human beings..." is equivalent to both of the following: "45 out of every 100 people..." "0.45 of the human population..." One way to think about percentages is to realize that "one percent", represented by the symbol %, is simply the number 1/100, or 0.01.
   a. -equivalence
   b. Percent12
   c. Undefined
   d. Undefined

22. An _____ is represented by two expressions that have the same value.
   a. ADE classification
   b. Equation12
   c. Undefined
   d. Undefined

23. When a number is written with an exponent this number will be in _____.
   a. ADE classification
   b. Exponential form12
   c. Undefined
   d. Undefined

24. An _____ combines numbers, operators, and/or variables but contains no equal or inequality sign.
   a. Expression12
   b. ADE classification
   c. Undefined
   d. Undefined

25. A _____ is a class of simple functions where they are constructed using only multiplication and addition of terms.
   a. Polynomial12
   b. -equivalence
   c. Undefined
   d. Undefined

Chapter 12. Discrete Mathematics: Statistics

26. A _____ is a series of points the same distance from a given point, called the center.
    a. -equivalence
    b. Circle12
    c. Undefined
    d. Undefined

27. The word _____ can have three meanings: In _____ theory, a _____ is an abstract object consisting of vertices (or nodes) and edges (or arcs) between pairs of vertices. The _____ of a function f : X ˝ Y is the set of all pairs (x,f(x)) The _____ of a relation, a generalisation of the _____ of a function.
    a. -equivalence
    b. Graph12
    c. Undefined
    d. Undefined

28. A _____, or bar chart, shows the values of the variable (or an interval of values) on the horizontal axis (abcissa or X-axis) and the heights of the bars above each value represents their frequencies of occurrence (the value on the ordinate or Y-axis).
    a. Histogram12
    b. -equivalence
    c. Undefined
    d. Undefined

29. In statistics an arrangement of values of a variable showing their observed or theoretical frequency of occurrence is called a _____.
    a. -equivalence
    b. Distribution12
    c. Undefined
    d. Undefined

30. Vertical axis of display containing the leading digits is referred to as _____.
    a. -equivalence
    b. Stem12
    c. Undefined
    d. Undefined

31. Horizontal axis of display containing the trailing digits is called _____.
    a. -equivalence
    b. Leaves12
    c. Undefined
    d. Undefined

32. An _____ is one of the number lines found on the rectangular coordinate system. The x asis is the horizontal number line while the y _____ is the vertical number line.
    a. ADE classification
    b. Axis12
    c. Undefined
    d. Undefined

33. A _____ is an undefined term. However, it is often thought of as a series of points. A _____ has one dimension - length. A _____ is either named by a lower case letter or by two points on the _____.
    a. Line12
    b. -equivalence
    c. Undefined
    d. Undefined

34. A measure of variability, the _____ is the distance from the lowest to the highest score.
    a. -equivalence
    b. Range12
    c. Undefined
    d. Undefined

Chapter 12. Discrete Mathematics: Statistics

35. A _____ provides a quantitative description of the likely occurrence of a particular event. _____ is conventionally expressed on a scale from 0 to 1; a rare event has a _____ close to 0, a very common event has a _____ close to 1. _____ is calculated as the ratio of the number of favorable events to the total number of possible events.
   a. Probability12
   b. -equivalence
   c. Undefined
   d. Undefined

36. _____ is another term for proportion; it is the value calculated by dividing the number of times an event occurs by the total number of times an experiment is carried out. The probability of an event can be thought of as its long-run _____ when an experiment is carried out many times.
   a. -equivalence
   b. Relative frequency12
   c. Undefined
   d. Undefined

37. It is often helpful to convert the frequencies of a frequency distribution into _____, which are the observed frequencies converted into percentages based on the total number of observations. The _____ tell us at a glance what percentage of the distribution had a particular value.
   a. Relative frequencies12
   b. -equivalence
   c. Undefined
   d. Undefined

38. The outcome of a trial is called the _____.
   a. Event12
   b. ADE classification
   c. Undefined
   d. Undefined

39. Two events are _____ when the occurrence of one precludes the occurrence of the other. Another word for _____ is disjoint.
   a. Mutually exclusive12
   b. -equivalence
   c. Undefined
   d. Undefined

40. Any time one number is on the left side of another number on a number line, the first number is _____ the second number. The symbol for this is <.
   a. -equivalence
   b. Less than12
   c. Undefined
   d. Undefined

41. An _____ is composed of two rays that have a common endpoint, called the vertex. Each _____ is named by a lower case letter or by one point from each ray and the vertex inbetween. _____ a might be the same _____ as _____ ABC.
   a. Angle12
   b. ADE classification
   c. Undefined
   d. Undefined

42. A _____ is a tool of measurement that measures the number of degrees in angles.
   a. Protractor12
   b. -equivalence
   c. Undefined
   d. Undefined

43. _____ means to multiply by 2.

Chapter 12. Discrete Mathematics: Statistics

    a. -equivalence
    b. Twice12
    c. Undefined
    d. Undefined

44. The number of times a particular score or event occurs with respect to the total number of events or scores is called its _____.
    a. Proportion12
    b. -equivalence
    c. Undefined
    d. Undefined

45. _____ is any number that multiples to get a product..
    a. -equivalence
    b. Factor12
    c. Undefined
    d. Undefined

46. factorization or _____ is the decomposition of an object (for example, a number, a polynomial, or a matrix) into a product of other objects, or factors, which when multiplied together give the original. For example, the number 15 factors into primes as 3 × 5; and the polynomial $x2 - 4$ factors as $(x - 2)(x + 2)$. In both cases, we obtain a product of simpler things.
    a. Factoring12
    b. -equivalence
    c. Undefined
    d. Undefined

47. _____ refers to the value that divides a sample of data into four groups containing an equal numbers of observations.
    a. Quartile12
    b. -equivalence
    c. Undefined
    d. Undefined

48. The answer to subtraction is called the _____.
    a. Difference12
    b. -equivalence
    c. Undefined
    d. Undefined

49. If one number is to the right of another number on the number line, this number is _____ the number on the left. The symbol that is used is >.
    a. -equivalence
    b. Greater than12
    c. Undefined
    d. Undefined

50. The _____ refers to the middle 50% of the observations. The _____ is often used in ordinal levels of measurement, such as surveys, to reduce the influence of extreme scores.
    a. ADE classification
    b. Interquartile range12
    c. Undefined
    d. Undefined

51. An extreme point that stands out from the rest of the distribution is called the _____.
    a. ADE classification
    b. Outlier12
    c. Undefined
    d. Undefined

52. The highest number in a list of values is called the _____.
    a. -equivalence
    b. Maximum12
    c. Undefined
    d. Undefined

53. The lowest number in a list of values is called the _____.

a. -equivalence
c. Undefined
b. Minimum12
d. Undefined

54. A graphical representation of the dispersion of a sample may be called a _____.
a. -equivalence
c. Undefined
b. Box-and-whisker plot12
d. Undefined

55. A _____ is a piece of a line. The _____ has definite length and is named by the two endpoints.
a. Line segment12
c. Undefined
b. -equivalence
d. Undefined

56. A quadrilateral with 4 equal sides and all right angles is called a _____.
a. Square12
c. Undefined
b. -equivalence
d. Undefined

57. A _____ is a relation where every x value has one and only y value.
a. Function12
c. Undefined
b. -equivalence
d. Undefined

58. The graph of a quadrataic equation is a symmetric curve called a _____.
a. Parabola12
c. Undefined
b. -equivalence
d. Undefined

59. A _____ is a concrete example of an item or a specification against which all others may be measured. For example, there are "primary standards" for length, mass (see Kilogram standard), and other units of measure, kept by laboratories and standards organizations.
a. -equivalence
c. Undefined
b. Standard12
d. Undefined

60. A _____ is the point that occurs whenever two lines, line segments, or rays meet. The _____ of an angle is very important.
a. -equivalence
c. Undefined
b. Vertex12
d. Undefined

61. A procedure for making logical decisions on the basis of sample data is commonly referred to as _____.
a. Decision-making12
c. Undefined
b. -equivalence
d. Undefined

62. A _____ is a scheme for the numerical representation of the values of a variable. The interpretation we place upon the numbers of the _____, rather than the numbers themselves, makes the _____ useful. The most common scales are nominal, ordinal, interval
a. Scale12
c. Undefined
b. -equivalence
d. Undefined

63. A _____ is an undefined term. We usually represent this by a dot, but a _____ actually has no dimension. A capital letter names any _____.

a. Point12
b. -equivalence
c. Undefined
d. Undefined

64. The degree to which individual data points are distributed around the mean is referred to as _____.
    a. Dispersion12
    b. -equivalence
    c. Undefined
    d. Undefined

65. A _____ refers to the distance or difference between any score in a distribution of data from the mean.
    a. Deviation12
    b. -equivalence
    c. Undefined
    d. Undefined

66. The same statistical principles apply to the evaluation of observed _____ between sets of data. The field of statistics provides the necessary techniques for making statements of our certainty that there are real as opposed to chance _____.
    a. Differences12
    b. -equivalence
    c. Undefined
    d. Undefined

67. A measure of variability in a distribution, the _____ is the square root of the variance. The _____ measures the variability of scores around the mean: the standardized difference. It is the square root of the mean square error.
    a. -equivalence
    b. Standard deviation12
    c. Undefined
    d. Undefined

68. The _____ is the a statistic which measures how spread out or dispersed a set of data is. It is The value calculated will always be greater than or equal to zero, with larger values corresponding to data which is more spread out. If all data values are identical, the _____ is equal to zero. The _____ is calculated as the mean square error: the sum of squared deviations about the mean, divided by the number of scores -1 degree of freedom.
    a. -equivalence
    b. Variance12
    c. Undefined
    d. Undefined

69. In a proportion the "middle" values are often referred to as the _____.
    a. -equivalence
    b. Means12
    c. Undefined
    d. Undefined

70. A _____ contains at least one squared term.
    a. Quadratic12
    b. -equivalence
    c. Undefined
    d. Undefined

71. A _____ is simply a polynomial with two terms such as this example: 2x + 7.
    a. -equivalence
    b. Binomial12
    c. Undefined
    d. Undefined

72. An _____ is any process or study, which results in the collection of data, the outcome of which is unknown. In statistics, the term is usually restricted to situations in which the researcher has control over some of the conditions under which the _____ takes place.

a. ADE classification
b. Experiment12
c. Undefined
d. Undefined

73. The number of successes in n independent trials that each have the same probability p of success has the _____ with parameters n and p. For example, the number of heads in 10 tosses of a fair coin has a _____ with parameters n=10 and p=50%. The expected value of the _____ is n×p , and the standard error of the _____ is (n×p×(1-p))½.
   a. -equivalence
   b. Binomial distribution12
   c. Undefined
   d. Undefined

74. A _____ is the relationship between two quantities. It is expressed as the quotient of two numbers, or as two numbers separated by a colon (pronounced "to"). A number that can be written as a _____ of two integers is a rational number.
   a. Ratio12
   b. -equivalence
   c. Undefined
   d. Undefined

75. The term _____ refers to a particular way in which observations will tend to pile up around a particular value rather than be spread evenly across a range of values. It is generally most applicable to continuous data and is intrinsically associated with parametric or inferential statistics. Graphically the _____ is best described by a bell-shaped curve. This curve is described in terms of the point at which its height is maximum, its mean, and how wide it is, its standard deviation.
   a. -equivalence
   b. Normal distribution12
   c. Undefined
   d. Undefined

76. In a large distribution of data it is often easier to understand the data if it is grouped into intervals where each _____ can contain more than one data value. Distributions are often reduced to 10 to 20 intervals.
   a. Interval12
   b. ADE classification
   c. Undefined
   d. Undefined

77. The outcome of an experiment need not be a number, for example, the outcome when a coin is tossed can be 'heads' or 'tails'. However, we often want to represent outcomes as numbers. A _____ is a function that associates a unique numerical value with every outcome of an experiment. The value of the random
   a. Random Variable12
   b. -equivalence
   c. Undefined
   d. Undefined

78. Any distribution can be converted to a standardized distribution. However the symmetry of the original distribution remains unchanged. If the original distribution was skewed to start with, it will still be skewed after the z-score transformation. In the special case where the original distribution can be considered normal, standardizing will result in what is known as the _____. A standardized normal distribution has a mean of 0 and standard deviation of 1.
   a. -equivalence
   b. Standard normal distribution12
   c. Undefined
   d. Undefined

79. The bottom part of any fraction represents the number of pieces in one whole unit. This bottom part is called the _____.
   a. Denominator12
   b. -equivalence
   c. Undefined
   d. Undefined

Chapter 12. Discrete Mathematics: Statistics

80. The very fact that we are measuring objects with respect to some characteristic implies that the objects differ in that characteristic; or stated in another way, that the characteristic can take on a number of different values. These properties or characteristics of an object that can assume two or more different values are referred to as a _____.
   a. Variable12
   b. -equivalence
   c. Undefined
   d. Undefined

81. The _____ refers to the amount of change in Y for a 1 unit change in X or is the ratio of the rise over the run; or in-other-words, the rate of change in the predicted value as a function of a change in the predictor variable.
   a. -equivalence
   b. Slope12
   c. Undefined
   d. Undefined

82. A _____ is an undefined term. We can think of it as a series of lines having 2 dimensions, width and length.
   a. Plane12
   b. -equivalence
   c. Undefined
   d. Undefined

83. The _____ of a graph or equation is the set of all the possible x values.
   a. -equivalence
   b. Domain12
   c. Undefined
   d. Undefined

84. A _____ is a number or variable, or the product or quotient of a number or variable.
   a. Term12
   b. -equivalence
   c. Undefined
   d. Undefined

85. The defining characteristics of populations are called _____. Observations must be made on every single member of the population in question in order to precisely state the value of _____.
   a. -equivalence
   b. Parameters12
   c. Undefined
   d. Undefined

Chapter 13. Trigonometric Functions

1. A piece of a circle is called an _____.
   a. Arc13
   b. ADE classification
   c. Undefined
   d. Undefined

2. Any polygon that has 3 sides is called a _____.
   a. Triangle13
   b. -equivalence
   c. Undefined
   d. Undefined

3. _____ is a branch of mathematics dealing with angles, triangles and trigonometric functions such as sine, cosine and tangent.
   a. Trigonometry13
   b. -equivalence
   c. Undefined
   d. Undefined

4. The amount of money paid for borrowing or investing money is called the _____. There are two main kinds of _____ called simple _____ and compound _____.
   a. ADE classification
   b. Interest13
   c. Undefined
   d. Undefined

5. An _____ is composed of two rays that have a common endpoint, called the vertex. Each _____ is named by a lower case letter or by one point from each ray and the vertex inbetween. _____ a might be the same _____ as _____ ABC.
   a. Angle13
   b. ADE classification
   c. Undefined
   d. Undefined

6. A _____ is an undefined term. However, it is often thought of as a series of points. A _____ has one dimension - length. A _____ is either named by a lower case letter or by two points on the _____.
   a. Line13
   b. -equivalence
   c. Undefined
   d. Undefined

7. _____ measure how long something is.
   a. Length13
   b. -equivalence
   c. Undefined
   d. Undefined

8. A _____ must contain a right angle.
   a. -equivalence
   b. Right triangle13
   c. Undefined
   d. Undefined

9. A variable is sometimes known as an _____.
   a. Unknown13
   b. ADE classification
   c. Undefined
   d. Undefined

10. A _____ occurs in a right triangle and is the side opposite the right angle. It will also be the longest side of a right triangle.
    a. -equivalence
    b. Hypotenuse13
    c. Undefined
    d. Undefined

Chapter 13. Trigonometric Functions

11. The _____ of a number is the number that makes a sum zero. In most cases, this means just to change the sign. 3 is the _____ of -3.
    a. Opposite13
    b. ADE classification
    c. Undefined
    d. Undefined

12. Any angle that equals 90 degrees is called a _____. This angle also forms perpendicular lines.
    a. Right angle13
    b. -equivalence
    c. Undefined
    d. Undefined

13. A angle that measures less than 90 degrees is called an _____.
    a. ADE classification
    b. Acute angle13
    c. Undefined
    d. Undefined

14. A _____ is the relationship between two quantities. It is expressed as the quotient of two numbers, or as two numbers separated by a colon (pronounced "to"). A number that can be written as a _____ of two integers is a rational number.
    a. -equivalence
    b. Ratio13
    c. Undefined
    d. Undefined

15. A _____ goes from left to right or from East to West.
    a. Horizontal line13
    b. -equivalence
    c. Undefined
    d. Undefined

16. A _____ is an undefined term. We usually represent this by a dot, but a _____ actually has no dimension. A capital letter names any _____.
    a. -equivalence
    b. Point13
    c. Undefined
    d. Undefined

17. Any set of ordered pairs is called a _____.
    a. Relation13
    b. -equivalence
    c. Undefined
    d. Undefined

18. The _____ refers to the amount of change in Y for a 1 unit change in X or is the ratio of the rise over the run; or in-other-words, the rate of change in the predicted value as a function of a change in the predictor variable.
    a. -equivalence
    b. Slope13
    c. Undefined
    d. Undefined

19. _____ (from the Greek words Geo = earth and metro = measure) is the branch of mathematics first popularized in ancient Greek culture by Thales (circa 624-547 BC) dealing with spatial relationships. The earliest beginnings of _____ may be traced to Ancient Egypt
    a. -equivalence
    b. Geometry13
    c. Undefined
    d. Undefined

Chapter 13. Trigonometric Functions

20. Addition (or summation) is one of the basic operations of arithmetic. In its simplest form, addition combines two numbers, the augend and addend, into a single number, the _____. Adding more numbers can be viewed as repeated addition. (Repeated addition of the number one is the most basic form of counting.) By extension, the addition of zero numbers, one number, or infinitely many numbers can be defined.
   a. -equivalence
   b. Sum13
   c. Undefined
   d. Undefined

21. Any polygon with 4 sides is called a _____. The sum of the interior angles is 360 degrees.
   a. Quadrilateral13
   b. -equivalence
   c. Undefined
   d. Undefined

22. A quadrilateral with opposite sides equal and parallel and containing all right angles is called a _____.
   a. -equivalence
   b. Rectangle13
   c. Undefined
   d. Undefined

23. A polygon with 6 sides is called a _____.
   a. Hexagon13
   b. -equivalence
   c. Undefined
   d. Undefined

24. A closed shape whose sides are all line segments is called a _____.
   a. -equivalence
   b. Polygon13
   c. Undefined
   d. Undefined

25. A _____ is a class of simple functions where they are constructed using only multiplication and addition of terms.
   a. -equivalence
   b. Polynomial13
   c. Undefined
   d. Undefined

26. The bottom part of any fraction represents the number of pieces in one whole unit. This bottom part is called the _____.
   a. Denominator13
   b. -equivalence
   c. Undefined
   d. Undefined

27. An _____ combines numbers, operators, and/or variables but contains no equal or inequality sign.
   a. ADE classification
   b. Expression13
   c. Undefined
   d. Undefined

28. A graphical representation of the dispersion of a sample may be called a _____.
   a. -equivalence
   b. Box-and-whisker plot13
   c. Undefined
   d. Undefined

29. By _____ we mean collecting observations made upon our environment -- observations, which are the results of measurements using clocks, balances, measuring rods, counting operations, or other objectively defined measuring instruments or procedures. _____ may mean simply counting the number of times a particular property occurs.
   a. -equivalence
   b. Data13
   c. Undefined
   d. Undefined

Chapter 13. Trigonometric Functions

30. The highest number in a list of values is called the _____.
    a. -equivalence
    b. Maximum13
    c. Undefined
    d. Undefined

31. The lowest number in a list of values is called the _____.
    a. Minimum13
    b. -equivalence
    c. Undefined
    d. Undefined

32. A _____ is a well-defined collection of objects considered as a whole.
    a. -equivalence
    b. Set13
    c. Undefined
    d. Undefined

33. A _____ is a series of points the same distance from a given point, called the center.
    a. Circle13
    b. -equivalence
    c. Undefined
    d. Undefined

34. The _____ of a circle is a chord that goes through the center.
    a. -equivalence
    b. Diameter13
    c. Undefined
    d. Undefined

35. The point of intersection of the horizontal and vertical axes in the rectangular coordinate plane is the _____. It is is expressed as the ordered pair (0,0).
    a. ADE classification
    b. Origin13
    c. Undefined
    d. Undefined

36. A _____ is an undefined term. We can think of it as a series of lines having 2 dimensions, width and length.
    a. Plane13
    b. -equivalence
    c. Undefined
    d. Undefined

37. An _____ is a point at the end of a line segment.
    a. ADE classification
    b. Endpoint13
    c. Undefined
    d. Undefined

38. A _____ is part of a line that starts with an endpoint and goes on in one direction only. It is named by the endpoint and any other point on the _____.
    a. Ray13
    b. -equivalence
    c. Undefined
    d. Undefined

39. A _____ is a concrete example of an item or a specification against which all others may be measured. For example, there are "primary standards" for length, mass (see Kilogram standard), and other units of measure, kept by laboratories and standards organizations.
    a. -equivalence
    b. Standard13
    c. Undefined
    d. Undefined

40. _____ are used to measure the size of angles. A circle has 360 _____ in it.

a. Degrees13
b. -equivalence
c. Undefined
d. Undefined

41. A measure of variability, the _____ is the distance from the lowest to the highest score.
    a. -equivalence
    b. Range13
    c. Undefined
    d. Undefined

42. The axes in a rectangular coordinate systems naturally cuts the plane into 4 separate regions called _____.These are usually represented by Roman Numerals starting with the upper right quadrant.
    a. Quadrants13
    b. -equivalence
    c. Undefined
    d. Undefined

43. A _____ is a relation where every x value has one and only y value.
    a. Function13
    b. -equivalence
    c. Undefined
    d. Undefined

44. An _____ is one of the number lines found on the rectangular coordinate system. The x asis is the horizontal number line while the y _____ is the vertical number line.
    a. ADE classification
    b. Axis13
    c. Undefined
    d. Undefined

45. Whenever you divide by zero the answer is _____.
    a. Undefined13
    b. ADE classification
    c. Undefined
    d. Undefined

46. The same statistical principles apply to the evaluation of observed _____ between sets of data. The field of statistics provides the necessary techniques for making statements of our certainty that there are real as opposed to chance _____.
    a. -equivalence
    b. Differences13
    c. Undefined
    d. Undefined

47. An _____ is represented by two expressions that have the same value.
    a. ADE classification
    b. Equation13
    c. Undefined
    d. Undefined

48. The word _____ can have three meanings: In _____ theory, a _____ is an abstract object consisting of vertices (or nodes) and edges (or arcs) between pairs of vertices. The _____ of a function f : X ¨ Y is the set of all pairs (x,f(x)) The _____ of a relation, a generalisation of the _____ of a function.
    a. -equivalence
    b. Graph13
    c. Undefined
    d. Undefined

49. One major objective of statistical analysis is the identification of associations or _____ that exist between and among sets of observations. In other words, does knowledge about about one set of data allow us to infer or predict characteristics about another set or sets of data.

Chapter 13. Trigonometric Functions

a. -equivalence
c. Undefined
b. Relationships13
d. Undefined

50. The _____ of a circle is the distance from the center to the circle.
a. -equivalence
c. Undefined
b. Radius13
d. Undefined

51. Since the observations in most data distributions tend to cluster heavily about certain values, one logical measure of central tendency would be that value which occurs most frequently; and that value is referred to as the _____ or modal value. For a nominal scale of measurement, the _____ is the best indicator of central tendency.
a. Mode13
c. Undefined
b. -equivalence
d. Undefined

52. The _____ of a graph or equation is the set of all the possible x values.
a. Domain13
c. Undefined
b. -equivalence
d. Undefined

53. A quadrilateral with 4 equal sides and all right angles is called a _____.
a. Square13
c. Undefined
b. -equivalence
d. Undefined

54. The most important measure of central tendency, and one of the basic building blocks of all statistical analysis, is the arithmetic _____. It is simply the sum of all the set of values divided by the number of values involved. It can also be called the average.
a. Mean13
c. Undefined
b. -equivalence
d. Undefined

55. A measure of central tendency, the _____, corresponds to the point having 50% of the observations below it when observations are arranged in numerical order. The _____ assumes at least an interval level of measurement. For a symmetric distribution such as the normal distribution, the _____ is the same as the mean. For a distribution which is skewed to the right, the _____ is typically smaller than the mean or when skewed to the left, the _____ is smaller.
a. -equivalence
c. Undefined
b. Median13
d. Undefined

56. A _____ refers to the distance or difference between any score in a distribution of data from the mean.
a. -equivalence
c. Undefined
b. Deviation13
d. Undefined

57. The _____ is the distance around a closed curve. _____ is a kind of perimeter.
a. Circumference13
c. Undefined
b. -equivalence
d. Undefined

58. A number that does not change in value in a given situation is a _____.
a. -equivalence
c. Undefined
b. Constant13
d. Undefined

Chapter 13. Trigonometric Functions

59. In a large distribution of data it is often easier to understand the data if it is grouped into intervals where each _____ can contain more than one data value. Distributions are often reduced to 10 to 20 intervals.
   a. ADE classification
   b. Interval13
   c. Undefined
   d. Undefined

60. A _____ goes up and down or from North to South.
   a. -equivalence
   b. Vertical line13
   c. Undefined
   d. Undefined

61. _____ is any number that multiples to get a product..
   a. Factor13
   b. -equivalence
   c. Undefined
   d. Undefined

62. The number of times a particular score or observation occurs is its _____.
   a. -equivalence
   b. Frequency13
   c. Undefined
   d. Undefined

63. _____ are intuitively defined as numbers that are in one-to-one correspondence with the points on an infinite line—the number line. The term "real number" is a retronym coined in response to "imaginary number" _____ may be rational or irrational; algebraic or transcendental; and positive, negative, or zero _____ measure continuous quantities. They may in theory be expressed by decimal fractions that have an infinite sequence of digits to the right of the decimal point; these are often (mis-)represented in the same form as 324.823211247... (where the three dots express that there would still be more digits to come, no matter how many more might be added at the end).
   a. Real numbers13
   b. -equivalence
   c. Undefined
   d. Undefined

64. When 2 or more equations are considered as a group, this creates a _____.
   a. System of equations13
   b. -equivalence
   c. Undefined
   d. Undefined

65. The amount of money borrowed or invested is called the _____.
   a. -equivalence
   b. Principal13
   c. Undefined
   d. Undefined

66. The first grouping symbol used are called _____ ( ).
   a. Parentheses13
   b. -equivalence
   c. Undefined
   d. Undefined

67. A number that is raised to a power, or _____ of an exponential function. This finds common use, for example, in the depiction of numbers, for instance, 10 is the _____ used in the decimal system, whereas 2 is the _____ in the binary numeral system.
   a. Base13
   b. -equivalence
   c. Undefined
   d. Undefined

Chapter 13. Trigonometric Functions

68. The goal of most inferential statistical analyses is to be able to generalize or apply the findings to the entire population and not just to the sample. The concept of _____ requires that the researcher determine some level of probability that the findings were due to chance or that they actually describe the population. The value of the probability that the findings were due to chance is usually reported when the findings of an analysis is reported.
   a. Generalization13
   b. -equivalence
   c. Undefined
   d. Undefined

69. _____ is the result of assigning numbers to objects to abstractly represent the objects or characteristics of the objects.
   a. -equivalence
   b. Measurement13
   c. Undefined
   d. Undefined

70. A _____ contains at least one squared term.
   a. Quadratic13
   b. -equivalence
   c. Undefined
   d. Undefined

71. A _____ is the answer in multiplication, or an expression that identifies factors to be multiplied
   a. Product13
   b. -equivalence
   c. Undefined
   d. Undefined

Chapter 14. Further Topics in Trigonometry

1. A quadrilateral with 4 equal sides and all right angles is called a _____.
   a. Square14
   b. -equivalence
   c. Undefined
   d. Undefined

2. An _____ is composed of two rays that have a common endpoint, called the vertex. Each _____ is named by a lower case letter or by one point from each ray and the vertex inbetween. _____ a might be the same _____ as _____ ABC.
   a. ADE classification
   b. Angle14
   c. Undefined
   d. Undefined

3. Any polygon that has 3 sides is called a _____.
   a. -equivalence
   b. Triangle14
   c. Undefined
   d. Undefined

4. A measure of variability, the _____ is the distance from the lowest to the highest score.
   a. Range14
   b. -equivalence
   c. Undefined
   d. Undefined

5. The word _____ can have three meanings: In _____ theory, a _____ is an abstract object consisting of vertices (or nodes) and edges (or arcs) between pairs of vertices. The _____ of a function f : X ¨ Y is the set of all pairs (x,f(x)) The _____ of a relation, a generalisation of the _____ of a function.
   a. Graph14
   b. -equivalence
   c. Undefined
   d. Undefined

6. The _____ says that in a right triangle, when you square the first leg and add this to the second leg squared you are then equal to the hypotenuse squared.
   a. -equivalence
   b. Pythagorean Theorem14
   c. Undefined
   d. Undefined

7. _____ measure how long something is.
   a. -equivalence
   b. Length14
   c. Undefined
   d. Undefined

8. A variable is sometimes known as an _____.
   a. Unknown14
   b. ADE classification
   c. Undefined
   d. Undefined

9. The _____ of a number is the number that makes a sum zero. In most cases, this means just to change the sign. 3 is the _____ of -3.
   a. ADE classification
   b. Opposite14
   c. Undefined
   d. Undefined

10. A number that is raised to a power, or _____ of an exponential function. This finds common use, for example, in the depiction of numbers, for instance, 10 is the _____ used in the decimal system, whereas 2 is the _____ in the binary numeral system.

Chapter 14. Further Topics in Trigonometry

a. Base14
b. -equivalence
c. Undefined
d. Undefined

11. _____ (from the Greek words Geo = earth and metro = measure) is the branch of mathematics first popularized in ancient Greek culture by Thales (circa 624-547 BC) dealing with spatial relationships. The earliest beginnings of _____ may be traced to Ancient Egypt

a. -equivalence
b. Geometry14
c. Undefined
d. Undefined

12. A triangle that has two equal sides is called an _____.

a. ADE classification
b. Isosceles triangle14
c. Undefined
d. Undefined

13. Any time one number is on the left side of another number on a number line, the first number is _____ the second number. The symbol for this is <.

a. -equivalence
b. Less than14
c. Undefined
d. Undefined

14. An _____ is represented by two expressions that have the same value.

a. Equation14
b. ADE classification
c. Undefined
d. Undefined

15. A _____ contains at least one squared term.

a. Quadratic14
b. -equivalence
c. Undefined
d. Undefined

16. A _____ is a relation where every x value has one and only y value.

a. -equivalence
b. Function14
c. Undefined
d. Undefined

17. Since the observations in most data distributions tend to cluster heavily about certain values, one logical measure of central tendency would be that value which occurs most frequently; and that value is referred to as the _____ or modal value. For a nominal scale of measurement, the _____ is the best indicator of central tendency.

a. -equivalence
b. Mode14
c. Undefined
d. Undefined

18. A _____ is the relationship between two quantities. It is expressed as the quotient of two numbers, or as two numbers separated by a colon (pronounced "to"). A number that can be written as a _____ of two integers is a rational number.

a. -equivalence
b. Ratio14
c. Undefined
d. Undefined

19. A _____ is a number that when multiplied by a given number gives you one. This is also called multiplicative inverse.

a. Reciprocal14
b. -equivalence
c. Undefined
d. Undefined

20. The answer to subtraction is called the _____.
   a. -equivalence
   b. Difference14
   c. Undefined
   d. Undefined

21. A _____ is a scheme for the numerical representation of the values of a variable. The interpretation we place upon the numbers of the _____, rather than the numbers themselves, makes the _____ useful. The most common scales are nominal, ordinal, interval
   a. Scale14
   b. -equivalence
   c. Undefined
   d. Undefined

22. A _____ is the point that occurs whenever two lines, line segments, or rays meet. The _____ of an angle is very important.
   a. -equivalence
   b. Vertex14
   c. Undefined
   d. Undefined

23. The point of intersection of the horizontal and vertical axes in the rectangular coordinate plane is the _____. It is is expressed as the ordered pair (0,0).
   a. ADE classification
   b. Origin14
   c. Undefined
   d. Undefined

24. Addition (or summation) is one of the basic operations of arithmetic. In its simplest form, addition combines two numbers, the augend and addend, into a single number, the _____. Adding more numbers can be viewed as repeated addition. (Repeated addition of the number one is the most basic form of counting.) By extension, the addition of zero numbers, one number, or infinitely many numbers can be defined.
   a. -equivalence
   b. Sum14
   c. Undefined
   d. Undefined

25. An _____ combines numbers, operators, and/or variables but contains no equal or inequality sign.
   a. ADE classification
   b. Expression14
   c. Undefined
   d. Undefined

26. The _____ of a graph or equation is the set of all the possible x values.
   a. -equivalence
   b. Domain14
   c. Undefined
   d. Undefined

27. Whenever a number is not divisible by 2, then it is called an _____ number.
   a. ADE classification
   b. Odd14
   c. Undefined
   d. Undefined

28. Any number that is divisible by 2 is an _____ number.
   a. Even14
   b. ADE classification
   c. Undefined
   d. Undefined

Chapter 14. Further Topics in Trigonometry

29. _____ is a quick way of adding identical numbers. For example, the sum 7 + 7 + 7 can be found by multiplying 3 times 7. This model is reflected in the use of the word times as a synonym for multiplied by. The resuult of multiplying numbers is called a product. The numbers being multiplied are called factors.
   a. Multiplication14
   b. -equivalence
   c. Undefined
   d. Undefined

30. A _____ is an undefined term. We can think of it as a series of lines having 2 dimensions, width and length.
   a. -equivalence
   b. Plane14
   c. Undefined
   d. Undefined

31. A _____ is an undefined term. We usually represent this by a dot, but a _____ actually has no dimension. A capital letter names any _____.
   a. -equivalence
   b. Point14
   c. Undefined
   d. Undefined

32. A _____ is the answer in multiplication, or an expression that identifies factors to be multiplied
   a. -equivalence
   b. Product14
   c. Undefined
   d. Undefined

33. In a large distribution of data it is often easier to understand the data if it is grouped into intervals where each _____ can contain more than one data value. Distributions are often reduced to 10 to 20 intervals.
   a. ADE classification
   b. Interval14
   c. Undefined
   d. Undefined

34. _____ is a branch of mathematics dealing with angles, triangles and trigonometric functions such as sine, cosine and tangent.
   a. Trigonometry14
   b. -equivalence
   c. Undefined
   d. Undefined

35. The very fact that we are measuring objects with respect to some characteristic implies that the objects differ in that characteristic; or stated in another way, that the characteristic can take on a number of different values. These properties or characteristics of an object that can assume two or more different values are referred to as a _____.
   a. -equivalence
   b. Variable14
   c. Undefined
   d. Undefined

36. _____ are characteristics or properties of an object that can take on one or more different values.
   a. Variables14
   b. -equivalence
   c. Undefined
   d. Undefined

37. _____ is a branch of mathematics which studies structure and quantity. It may be roughly characterized as a generalization and abstraction of arithmetic, in which operations are performed on symbols rather than numbers. It includes elementary _____, taught to high school students, as well as abstract _____ which covers such structures as groups, rings and fields. Along with geometry and analysis, it is one of the three principal branches of mathematics.
   a. ADE classification
   b. Algebra14
   c. Undefined
   d. Undefined

38. _____ measures how heavy or light something is.
   a. -equivalence
   b. Weight14
   c. Undefined
   d. Undefined

39. A _____ is a series of points the same distance from a given point, called the center.
   a. Circle14
   b. -equivalence
   c. Undefined
   d. Undefined

40. A piece of a circle is called an _____.
   a. Arc14
   b. ADE classification
   c. Undefined
   d. Undefined

41. Any polygon with 4 sides is called a _____. The sum of the interior angles is 360 degrees.
   a. Quadrilateral14
   b. -equivalence
   c. Undefined
   d. Undefined

42. _____ is a measure of how close an estimator is expected to be to the true value of a parameter.
   a. Precision14
   b. -equivalence
   c. Undefined
   d. Undefined

43. The _____ of a circle is the distance from the center to the circle.
   a. -equivalence
   b. Radius14
   c. Undefined
   d. Undefined

44. A _____ provides a quantitative description of the likely occurrence of a particular event. _____ is conventionally expressed on a scale from 0 to 1; a rare event has a _____ close to 0, a very common event has a _____ close to 1. _____ is calculated as the ratio of the number of favorable events to the total number of possible events.
   a. Probability14
   b. -equivalence
   c. Undefined
   d. Undefined

45. _____ are used to measure the size of angles. A circle has 360 _____ in it.
   a. -equivalence
   b. Degrees14
   c. Undefined
   d. Undefined

46. When something occurs once a year it is said to occur _____.
   a. Annually14
   b. ADE classification
   c. Undefined
   d. Undefined

47. The amount of money paid for borrowing or investing money is called the _____. There are two main kinds of _____ called simple _____ and compound _____.
   a. ADE classification
   b. Interest14
   c. Undefined
   d. Undefined

ANSWER KEY

Chapter 1

1. b	2. a	3. a	4. a	5. a	6. b	7. b	8. b	9. a	10. a
11. b	12. a	13. b	14. a	15. b	16. b	17. a	18. a	19. a	20. b
21. b	22. a	23. b	24. a	25. b	26. a	27. a	28. b	29. b	30. b
31. b	32. b	33. b	34. a	35. b	36. b	37. a	38. b	39. b	40. a
41. a	42. b	43. a	44. a	45. b	46. a	47. a	48. a	49. b	50. b
51. a	52. a	53. a	54. a	55. b	56. b	57. b	58. b	59. b	60. a
61. b	62. a	63. a	64. a	65. a	66. a	67. b	68. a	69. b	70. b
71. a	72. b	73. a	74. b	75. a	76. a	77. a	78. b	79. b	80. a
81. a	82. a	83. b	84. a	85. a	86. b	87. a	88. a	89. b	90. b
91. b	92. b	93. b	94. a	95. b	96. a	97. b	98. b	99. b	100. a
101. a	102. b	103. a	104. b	105. a	106. b	107. b	108. a	109. a	110. a
111. b	112. b	113. a	114. b	115. a	116. a	117. b	118. a	119. b	120. a
121. b	122. b	123. a	124. b	125. b	126. a	127. a	128. b	129. a	130. a
131. b	132. b	133. a	134. a	135. a	136. a	137. a	138. a	139. b	140. b
141. b	142. a	143. a	144. a	145. a	146. b				

Chapter 2

1. a	2. b	3. b	4. b	5. a	6. a	7. b	8. b	9. a	10. b
11. a	12. b	13. b	14. b	15. b	16. a	17. b	18. a	19. a	20. a
21. b	22. a	23. b	24. a	25. a	26. a	27. a	28. a	29. b	30. a
31. b	32. a	33. a	34. b	35. a	36. b	37. b	38. a	39. a	40. a
41. b	42. b	43. a	44. b	45. a	46. a	47. b	48. b	49. a	50. a
51. b	52. b	53. a	54. a	55. b	56. a	57. a	58. b	59. b	60. b
61. a	62. a	63. b	64. a	65. b	66. a	67. b	68. b	69. a	70. a
71. b	72. b	73. a	74. b	75. b	76. a	77. a	78. b	79. a	80. a
81. a	82. b	83. b	84. a	85. b	86. a	87. a	88. a	89. a	90. a
91. a	92. b	93. a	94. b	95. a	96. b	97. b	98. b	99. a	100. a
101. b	102. b	103. a	104. b	105. b	106. a	107. b	108. b	109. a	110. b
111. a	112. a	113. b	114. b	115. a	116. a	117. b	118. b	119. a	120. b
121. b	122. b	123. b	124. a	125. a	126. a	127. a	128. a	129. b	130. b
131. b	132. a	133. b	134. a	135. b	136. a	137. a	138. a	139. b	140. b
141. a	142. b	143. a	144. b	145. a	146. a	147. a	148. a	149. b	150. b
151. b	152. a	153. a	154. b	155. a	156. a	157. b	158. a	159. a	160. b
161. a	162. b	163. a	164. b	165. b					

Chapter 3

1. b	2. a	3. a	4. a	5. a	6. b	7. b	8. a	9. a	10. b
11. b	12. b	13. a	14. b	15. b	16. a	17. a	18. a	19. b	20. b
21. a	22. a	23. a	24. a	25. b	26. b	27. b	28. b	29. b	30. b
31. b	32. a	33. a	34. a	35. b	36. a	37. a	38. b	39. b	40. a
41. a	42. b	43. b	44. a	45. b	46. a	47. b	48. b	49. b	50. b
51. b	52. a	53. b	54. b	55. b	56. a	57. b	58. b	59. a	60. a
61. a	62. b	63. b	64. a	65. b	66. b	67. a	68. a	69. b	70. a
71. b	72. a	73. a	74. b	75. a	76. a	77. a	78. a	79. b	80. b
81. a	82. a	83. b	84. b	85. a	86. a	87. b	88. b	89. b	90. a
91. a	92. a	93. a	94. b	95. b	96. b	97. b	98. a	99. a	100. a
101. a	102. a	103. a	104. b	105. a	106. b	107. a	108. a	109. a	110. a
111. b	112. b	113. a	114. a	115. b	116. a				

Chapter 4

1. a	2. a	3. a	4. b	5. a	6. a	7. a	8. b	9. a	10. b
11. b	12. b	13. b	14. b	15. b	16. b	17. b	18. b	19. a	20. b
21. b	22. b	23. a	24. b	25. a	26. b	27. b	28. a	29. b	30. b
31. a	32. a	33. a	34. b	35. a	36. b	37. b	38. b	39. b	40. b
41. b	42. b	43. b	44. a	45. a	46. a	47. b	48. b	49. b	50. b
51. a	52. b	53. b	54. a	55. b	56. a	57. a	58. b	59. a	60. a
61. a	62. b	63. b	64. a	65. a	66. a	67. b	68. a	69. b	70. a
71. b	72. a	73. a	74. a	75. a	76. b	77. a	78. a	79. b	80. a
81. a	82. a	83. b	84. b	85. a	86. a	87. a	88. b	89. a	90. b
91. b	92. a	93. b	94. b	95. a	96. b	97. b	98. a	99. a	100. a
101. a	102. b								

Chapter 5

1. a	2. a	3. b	4. a	5. b	6. a	7. b	8. a	9. a	10. b
11. a	12. b	13. b	14. a	15. b	16. b	17. b	18. a	19. b	20. a
21. b	22. a	23. b	24. b	25. a	26. a	27. b	28. b	29. b	30. a
31. a	32. b	33. a	34. a	35. b	36. a	37. b	38. a	39. a	40. b
41. a	42. b	43. a	44. b	45. b	46. a	47. a	48. a	49. b	50. b
51. a	52. b	53. b	54. b	55. b	56. b	57. a	58. a	59. a	60. b
61. a	62. a	63. b	64. a	65. a	66. b	67. a	68. b	69. b	70. a
71. b	72. b	73. a	74. a	75. a	76. b	77. a	78. b	79. b	80. b
81. b	82. b	83. b	84. a	85. a	86. b	87. a	88. b	89. a	90. b
91. b	92. a	93. a	94. a	95. a	96. b	97. a	98. a	99. b	100. a
101. b	102. a	103. a	104. b	105. b	106. b	107. a	108. a	109. a	110. a
111. b	112. b	113. b	114. a	115. b	116. b	117. a	118. b	119. b	120. b
121. a	122. a	123. a	124. a	125. b	126. a	127. a	128. a	129. a	130. b
131. a	132. b	133. a	134. b	135. a	136. a	137. b	138. a	139. b	140. a
141. b	142. b	143. b	144. b	145. b	146. a	147. b	148. b	149. b	150. a
151. a									

ANSWER KEY

Chapter 6

1. b	2. a	3. a	4. a	5. b	6. b	7. a	8. b	9. a	10. b
11. a	12. a	13. a	14. a	15. b	16. b	17. b	18. b	19. b	20. b
21. a	22. a	23. a	24. b	25. b	26. a	27. a	28. b	29. b	30. a
31. a	32. a	33. b	34. b	35. b	36. a	37. a	38. b	39. a	40. a
41. b	42. a	43. b	44. b	45. b	46. b	47. b	48. a	49. a	50. b
51. a	52. b	53. b	54. a	55. b	56. a	57. a	58. b	59. a	60. b
61. a	62. b	63. b	64. a	65. a	66. b	67. a	68. a	69. b	70. b
71. b	72. a	73. b	74. b	75. b	76. b	77. a	78. a	79. a	80. b
81. b	82. b	83. b	84. a	85. a	86. b	87. a	88. a	89. b	90. a
91. b	92. a	93. a	94. a	95. b	96. a	97. b	98. b	99. a	100. b
101. a	102. a	103. b	104. a	105. a	106. b	107. b	108. b	109. b	110. b
111. b	112. a	113. a	114. a	115. a	116. a	117. b	118. b	119. b	120. a
121. a	122. a	123. b	124. b	125. a	126. a	127. b	128. b	129. b	130. b
131. b	132. b	133. b	134. a	135. b	136. a	137. a	138. b	139. a	140. a

Chapter 7

1. b	2. a	3. a	4. a	5. a	6. a	7. a	8. a	9. a	10. b
11. b	12. b	13. b	14. a	15. b	16. b	17. a	18. a	19. a	20. a
21. a	22. a	23. b	24. a	25. b	26. b	27. b	28. a	29. a	30. a
31. a	32. a	33. b	34. a	35. b	36. b	37. a	38. a	39. a	40. b
41. b	42. b	43. a	44. b	45. b	46. a	47. b	48. b	49. a	50. a
51. b	52. b	53. b	54. a	55. b	56. b	57. b	58. a	59. a	60. a
61. b	62. b	63. b	64. b	65. b	66. b	67. b	68. a	69. b	70. a
71. b	72. b	73. b	74. b	75. a	76. a	77. a	78. a	79. b	80. a
81. b	82. a	83. a	84. a	85. b	86. a	87. a	88. a	89. b	90. b
91. a	92. a	93. b	94. a	95. b	96. a	97. a	98. a	99. a	100. b
101. a	102. a	103. b	104. b	105. a	106. b	107. a	108. b	109. b	110. a
111. b	112. b	113. a	114. a	115. b	116. b	117. a	118. b	119. a	120. a
121. b	122. b	123. a	124. a	125. a	126. a	127. a	128. a	129. a	130. a

Chapter 8

1. b	2. b	3. a	4. a	5. a	6. b	7. b	8. a	9. b	10. a
11. b	12. b	13. b	14. a	15. a	16. a	17. a	18. b	19. a	20. a
21. a	22. a	23. a	24. a	25. b	26. b	27. b	28. a	29. b	30. b
31. a	32. a	33. b	34. b	35. b	36. b	37. b	38. a	39. b	40. b
41. b	42. b	43. a	44. a	45. b	46. b	47. a	48. b	49. b	50. a
51. a	52. b	53. b	54. b	55. a	56. b	57. a	58. b	59. a	60. a
61. b	62. b	63. a	64. b	65. a	66. b	67. b	68. a	69. a	70. b
71. b	72. a	73. a	74. a	75. b	76. b	77. a	78. b	79. b	80. a
81. a	82. b	83. a	84. a	85. b	86. a	87. b	88. b	89. b	90. b
91. b	92. a	93. b	94. a	95. b	96. b	97. a	98. a	99. a	100. b
101. b	102. b	103. a	104. b	105. b	106. b	107. b	108. a	109. b	110. b
111. b	112. b	113. a	114. b	115. a	116. a	117. a	118. b	119. b	120. b
121. a	122. b	123. a	124. b	125. a	126. b	127. b	128. a	129. a	130. b
131. a	132. b	133. a	134. a	135. a	136. b	137. b	138. a	139. a	140. b
141. b	142. b	143. b	144. a	145. a	146. b	147. a	148. b	149. a	150. b
151. b	152. a	153. b	154. b	155. a	156. b	157. b	158. a	159. b	160. a
161. b	162. b								

Chapter 9

1. a	2. a	3. a	4. a	5. b	6. b	7. b	8. a	9. b	10. a
11. a	12. b	13. b	14. a	15. a	16. b	17. b	18. b	19. b	20. b
21. a	22. a	23. b	24. a	25. b	26. b	27. b	28. b	29. a	30. b
31. a	32. a	33. b	34. b	35. b	36. a	37. b	38. b	39. b	40. a
41. a	42. b	43. a	44. a	45. a	46. a	47. a	48. a	49. a	50. b
51. b	52. b	53. a	54. b	55. b	56. a	57. b	58. b	59. a	60. a
61. a	62. a	63. b	64. b	65. a	66. a	67. a	68. a	69. a	70. a
71. b	72. b	73. a	74. a	75. a	76. a	77. a	78. b	79. a	80. a
81. a	82. b	83. b	84. a	85. a	86. a	87. b	88. a	89. b	90. b
91. b	92. a	93. a	94. a	95. a	96. b	97. b	98. b	99. a	100. a
101. a	102. a	103. a	104. b	105. a	106. a	107. b	108. b	109. a	110. b
111. b	112. a	113. b	114. b	115. b	116. b	117. b	118. b	119. b	120. b
121. b	122. b	123. b	124. a	125. a	126. b	127. a	128. a	129. b	130. a
131. a									

Chapter 10

1. b	2. a	3. b	4. b	5. a	6. b	7. b	8. a	9. b	10. b
11. b	12. b	13. b	14. a	15. b	16. b	17. a	18. a	19. a	20. a
21. a	22. b	23. a	24. b	25. a	26. b	27. b	28. a	29. b	30. a
31. b	32. a	33. b	34. a	35. a	36. b	37. b	38. a	39. a	40. b
41. b	42. a	43. b	44. a	45. b	46. b	47. b	48. a	49. a	50. a
51. b	52. a	53. a	54. a	55. a	56. a	57. b			

ANSWER KEY

Chapter 11

1. a	2. b	3. b	4. b	5. b	6. a	7. a	8. b	9. a	10. a
11. b	12. b	13. b	14. b	15. a	16. b	17. a	18. b	19. a	20. a
21. a	22. b	23. b	24. b	25. b	26. a	27. a	28. b	29. a	30. a
31. b	32. a	33. b	34. a	35. b	36. a	37. b	38. a	39. b	40. a
41. a	42. b	43. a	44. a	45. a	46. a	47. b	48. b	49. b	50. a
51. a	52. b	53. b	54. b	55. a	56. b	57. b	58. b	59. b	60. a
61. a	62. b	63. a	64. b	65. b	66. b	67. a	68. b		

Chapter 12

1. b	2. a	3. a	4. b	5. a	6. b	7. b	8. a	9. a	10. b
11. a	12. a	13. b	14. a	15. b	16. a	17. b	18. b	19. a	20. b
21. b	22. b	23. b	24. a	25. a	26. b	27. b	28. a	29. b	30. b
31. b	32. b	33. a	34. b	35. a	36. b	37. a	38. a	39. a	40. b
41. a	42. a	43. b	44. a	45. b	46. a	47. a	48. a	49. b	50. b
51. b	52. b	53. b	54. b	55. a	56. a	57. a	58. a	59. b	60. b
61. a	62. a	63. a	64. a	65. a	66. a	67. b	68. b	69. b	70. a
71. b	72. b	73. b	74. a	75. b	76. a	77. a	78. b	79. a	80. a
81. b	82. a	83. b	84. a	85. b					

Chapter 13

1. a	2. a	3. a	4. b	5. a	6. a	7. a	8. b	9. a	10. b
11. a	12. a	13. b	14. b	15. a	16. b	17. a	18. b	19. b	20. b
21. a	22. b	23. a	24. b	25. b	26. a	27. b	28. b	29. b	30. b
31. a	32. b	33. a	34. b	35. b	36. a	37. b	38. a	39. b	40. a
41. b	42. a	43. a	44. b	45. a	46. b	47. b	48. b	49. b	50. b
51. a	52. a	53. a	54. a	55. b	56. b	57. a	58. b	59. b	60. b
61. a	62. b	63. a	64. a	65. b	66. a	67. a	68. a	69. b	70. a
71. a									

Chapter 14

1. a	2. b	3. b	4. a	5. a	6. b	7. b	8. a	9. b	10. a
11. b	12. b	13. b	14. a	15. a	16. b	17. b	18. b	19. a	20. b
21. a	22. b	23. b	24. b	25. b	26. b	27. b	28. a	29. a	30. b
31. b	32. b	33. b	34. a	35. b	36. a	37. b	38. b	39. a	40. a
41. a	42. a	43. b	44. a	45. b	46. a	47. b			